prayingtogether

Equipping small groups
to grow their prayer potential

 Allan Harkness

Praying Together
Equipping small groups to grow their prayer potential

© Allan Harkness 2004

Published by Scripture Union,

Locked Bag 2, Central Coast BC NSW 2252, Australia, www.scriptureunion.org.au

207-209 Queensway, Bletchley, MK2 2EB, England, www.scriptureunion.org.uk

PO Box 760, Newtown, Wellington, New Zealand, www.scriptureunion.org.nz

7 Armenian St, #03-07 Bible House, Singapore 179932 www.su.org.sg

This book is a revision of *Praying Together: A handbook to encourage more effective prayer in small groups* (Scripture Union Australia/Joint Board of Christian Education, Melbourne, Australia: 1996).

A significant source of material for the original *Praying Together* was a series of prayer ideas published in several forms by Scripture Union New Zealand.

Scripture quotations marked (CEV) are from the Contemporary English Version © American Bible Society 1991, 1995.

Scripture quotations marked (GNT) are from the Good News Translation Revised Edition © American Bible Society 1966, 1971, 1976, 1992.

Scripture marked (NIV) is taken from the Holy Bible, New International Version® Copyright © 1973, 1978,1984 by International Bible Society. Used by permission of Zondervan. All rights reserved.

Scripture quotations marked (NLT) are taken from the Holy Bible, New Living Translation, copyright © 1996. Used by permission of Tyndale House Publishers, Inc., Wheaton, Illinois 60189. All rights reserved.

Scripture taken from The Message is Copyright © 1993, 1994, 1995, 1996, 2000, 2001, 2002. Used by permission NavPress Publishing Group.

National Library of Australia Cataloguing-in-publication entry
A catalogue record for this book is available from the National Library of Australia.

Design & Layout by RokatDesign.com.au

*Scripture Union is an international organisation working with churches in more than 130 countries providing resources to bring the good news about Jesus Christ to children, young people and families - and to encourage them to develop spiritually through the Bible and prayer. As well as our network of volunteers, staff and associates who run holidays, church-based events and school Christian groups, we produce a wide range of publications and support those who use our resources through training programmes.

contents

Are you in the picture?

Lunchtime. Highford Polytechnic. Fifteen members of the Christian fellowship have just finished a Bible study on effective faith-sharing. They have identified some fellow students who have been asking questions since seeing a recent Christian drama. The group members want God's perspectives on what to do now. Their leader says, 'Let's pray about what we have been discussing...'

9.48 pm. Meeting room, St. Christopher's Church. The monthly leaders' meeting is drawing to a close. There's been thoughtful discussion about church affairs, animated debate about whether they can afford both new carpet and a youth worker this year, concern expressed about some members' ill-health, and a brain-storm on ways to make more contact with people using the adjacent community centre. The chairman says, 'Well, that's our agenda for the evening. Let's pray to finish the meeting...'

10.21 am. Office cafeteria, a city high-rise office block. Bob, Julie, and Kenneth have been talking about their recent daily Bible readings in 1 Peter (using Scripture Union's *Closer to God*) in the light of imminent staff redundancies. They have a few minutes before they need to return to their desks, and Kenneth suggests, 'Let's take a few moments and pray about this...'

8.47 pm. Lounge, Alton Community Church. The weekly church prayer meeting is in progress. Alvin stifles a yawn and glances at his watch. Gwenda Oh is still praying, and Alvin can't remember what topics her prayer has covered. Suddenly he hears '...in Jesus' name, amen', and expects he should pray next. He opens his mouth, 'Dear God...'

11.34 am., Sunday. A classroom in Charis New Life Church. Elsie, who has recently recommitted her life to Christ, is petrified. She appreciates the weekly warm fellowship and relevant discussion in the 'Disciples today' small group, but when the leader invariably says, 'Let's pray around the group about what we've discovered this morning' Elsie freezes. There is a very loud silence, and Elsie's aware that she is the only one who hasn't yet prayed...

Change a few details in one or other of these scenarios, and do you see yourself or your Christians friends there? These are fairly common situations in which groups of people consciously want to share part of themselves with God. That is, they want to pray — with others.

4

prayer on the agenda
chapterone

Making prayer work

If you ask Christians around you what they struggle with most in their relationship with God, frequently 'making prayer work' comes near the top of the list. That's so for individuals – and usually more so for small groups of Christians.

Often prayer with others is marked by comments like these:

- 'It's so difficult to pray in a small group.'

- 'Praying in our group is predictable to the point of boredom.'

- 'Frankly, it borders on being irrelevant most of the time.'

- 'I pray aloud, but I don't know whether anyone else in the group really cares about what I'm saying.'

- 'It's the long silences I find so embarrassing.'

- 'It's OK – but is sharing conversation with God really supposed to be this mundane?'

Prayer in small groups needn't be like this!

What's in this book?

This book is designed to help you in group prayer to:
... recognise the common difficulties and challenges,
... acquire some of the skills needed to overcome these hurdles, and
... stimulate you to fresh and more ardent group prayer experiences.

Conversing with God together is important because for Christians, prayer is important and small groups are important. When prayer and small groups are combined, there is potential to make progress and to be creative in group prayer in ways we haven't imagined possible.

This book doesn't need to be read straight through from cover to cover. Browse through the contents (p3) to see what might be most helpful for your group. You will find:

Chapter 1: Putting prayer on the agenda.

Chapter 2: Discover the synergy that can result when you intentionally bring together the dynamics of prayer and small groups.

Chapter 3: This chapter takes a group, step-by-step, on a journey starting from where no one opens their mouths to pray, to effective conversational prayer with all involved.

Chapter 4: Start enhancing prayer in your small groups by picking ideas from this smorgasbord of creative methods, based on the well-known prayer framework of ACTS: Adoration, Confession, Thanksgiving and Supplication.

Chapter 5: More creative ideas, based on a wide range of prayer styles: written and published prayers, music and silence, multi-sensory prayer and using contemporary electronic media like the internet and mobile phones.

Chapter 6: This chapter highlights ways in which using the Bible and prayer together can make group communication with God more meaningful.

Chapter 7: There are many different sorts of small groups in which prayer can play a vital role. This chapter gives suggestions and hints for prayer in some of these groups.

Appendix: A list of resources to help you keep making headway in effective and creative prayer in your small groups.

The ideas in this book work best with a group of 8-12 people, for example a Bible study group or small fellowship group. However, they are adaptable to groups of other sizes, from a couple to a worshipping congregation.

Plan for effective group prayer

Effective group prayer seldom 'just happens'. Prayer does not come naturally to many groups. And – ironically – often groups which struggle most with meaningful group prayer are those made up of individuals who are quite proficient in personal prayer.

So, on your journey in group prayer, keep in mind four key principles.

1. Effective prayer in small groups is a skill to be learned.

Like all disciplines of the Christian life, prayer in small groups is something to be learned. It may mean learning a new attitude, but there are skills to be acquired, too.

For example, group participants need to learn the skills of listening carefully to one another, building on each others' contributions, and signalling that they are actively participating in what is being prayed by others.

Different methods are involved because people are wired differently in their personalities and how they express their relationship to God. All members won't feel equally comfortable praying aloud. There are no prizes for 'prayer clones', people who pray in identical fashion.

Group members may need to be encouraged to talk naturally about how they wish to pray together, be disciplined during the learning process, and then debrief on how it went. There is nothing unspiritual about lovingly correcting someone's prayer-style, consciously learning from what we've done well, along with our failures.

2. The best way to learn to pray in groups is to pray in groups!

Talking together about how to pray in our small groups will be helpful, but the best way to learn about prayer is by praying. Again, like other disciplines of Christian living, practice is important, and practice should be followed by careful review. At first, we may feel self-conscious and awkward using particular techniques, because it requires focusing on the method. But moving carefully through the discipline (yes, and enjoyment) of praying in a particular way will be more likely to bring us to a place where God can do his gracious work of transforming, nurturing, and challenging us. So creative enthusiasm and perseverance need to go hand-in-hand.

3.Effective group prayer needs to be planned.

It is far too easy for prayer to be squeezed out of small group life. This may be due to the priorities of the group, poor time management, or the pressure of trying to do too much in the group. But prayer is a vital avenue for relationship-building with God, and for expressing cooperative partnership in what he is doing, so energy and time should be invested, to ensure that it happens – and happens well.

So talk in your group about the place given to prayer. Make the tough decisions, and then use insights and ideas from this book to plan to achieve your agreed goals for group prayer.

4.Planning encourages sensitivity to the Holy Spirit

People who find it hard to modify their prayer-style in groups may claim that 'learning prayer techniques will restrict God's Spirit.' Recognise that, at first, such people may feel inhibited. But giving suggestions about how to pray is little different from suggesting how to structure other aspects of small group life, such as Bible study methods and worship. The ideas suggested are not meant to compete with, or override, the work of the Holy Spirit, rather, they may provide a setting which enhances a greater sensitivity to his work in the group and in its members. This shouldn't surprise us, when we realise that our Creator God enables his people to be creative in their communication with him.

There is nothing magical about prayer. 'Successful prayer' is not assured by any specific methods or skills. However, the experience of many small groups is that when they creatively structure their prayer experiences, they discover themselves opening up to God in new ways. Often, to their surprise, they move further than they imagined possible, in fulfilling God's purpose for them.

That could be the same for your group, as you use this book to stimulate your journey with God.

small groups & prayer: dynamic partnership

chaptertwo

Many Christians have discovered a special dynamic when they pray. As they see God working out his purposes more effectively, their commitment to God deepens and they are encouraged to 'keep going' as Jesus' disciples.

In both individual and group prayer, the same act takes place (coming into the presence of the living God and spending time with him) but this dynamic is different when Christians pray with others. When we pray with other people, we need to create prayer that reflects the perspectives and focus of the group as a whole. *Together* we seek to move into that vital relationship with God that is meant for our mutual enjoyment and enrichment.

It is good to take some time to review why prayer and small groups are important for Christians, and then to note some of the potential dynamics when they are integrated.

Why is prayer important?

The Christian life is all about relationships. When Jesus was asked which commandment was the most important, he answered not with 'don't do this...' or 'don't do that...'. Instead he said,

The most important one says: '...you have only one Lord and God. You must love him with all your heart, soul, mind, and strength.' The second most important commandment says: 'Love others as much as you love yourself.' No other commandment is more important than these.

Mark 12:29-31(CEV)

Love God ... and love your neighbour. And **prayer** is a key means by which we demonstrate our commitment to these two relationships.

What is prayer?

People are likely to give a variety of responses to this question. For example:

- 'Prayer is talking to God.'

- 'Prayer is asking God for what I need.'

- 'Prayer is telling God how much we love him.'

- 'Prayer is praising God.'

Each of these contains part of what prayer is about, but they tend to reflect an activist perspective. Too often prayer is limited to something we *do* or *perform* – and afterwards we may not have too much to show for it. These responses also tend to show a fairly one-way flow of communication, from us to God. James Houston, a notable writer on prayer, puts it this way:

> *We are so used to talking at God that many of us are really practising ventriloquists – we have all this one-way communication and he seems to be awfully silent in the process. The more we talk the less we seem to have any conviction that he's heard us – and the less satisfaction we gain from our times of prayer.*

Prayer as friendship with God

Consider this description of prayer, from a Christian many centuries ago, Teresa of Avila:

> *Prayer is nothing else than being on terms of friendship with God.*

Meaningful friendship with people involves getting to know them – who they really are, what they enjoy or dislike, and how they tick. But friendship is more than thinking about our friends or talking to them. Real friendship is based on 'affective knowledge', that is, knowledge that leads to loving, and responding to being loved.

It's the same with prayer. Another definition of prayer is that it is 'the raising of the heart and mind to God.' This recognises that prayer mustn't be mind-less, but that it needs to allow for persons to commune with each other. For Christians, this means allowing the Spirit of Jesus Christ to commune with our spirits. Such times of 'simply being in God's presence' are sometimes called contemplative prayer.

Prayer as partnership with God

This sort of prayer is more than performing a set of spiritual exercises. It is about how we respond to God, getting to know him, appreciate him and discover his perspective for our lives. In this respect prayer is:

- an expression of *faith*. When we pray we are saying to God, 'We know we are not God. By ourselves we can't achieve what we are praying about, so we trust you with our lives because you are God, and you know what is best. We want to understand more of your view of things.'
- an expression of *love*. When we pray we are saying to God, 'It's only because you love us that we are able to love you. It's your grace that makes us to want to submit ourselves to learn what you want for us. How can we express this?'
- an expression of *discipleship*. When we pray we are saying to God, 'Like Jesus, we want to be part of your kingdom in our world. We want to see you rule. We accept your invitation to work in your world through us.'

When we express our faith, love and willingness to serve in this way, God graciously releases his power and resources to us. God delights in the growing sense of community that springs up between him and his people, and accepts us as co-partners in the work of his kingdom. As John Guest puts it:

> *It is remarkable to think that God has given us a partnership with him in directing the course of human events. It is extraordinary to realize that our prayer can change events and circumstances in the world around us.*
>
> (from *Finding Deeper Intimacy with God: Only a Prayer Away*, Baker Books. Used by permission.)

How does this work? When we spend time with God, we are able to seek and discover his will, rather than imposing our demands on him.

We look back, and discover that what occupies us more and more is what brings him honour and glory.

But as that happens, we find – remarkably – that we are changing, too. And we discover that as we open up ourselves to God in prayer, we become the answer to our own prayers. Richard Foster has put it this way:

> To pray is to change. Prayer is the central avenue God uses to transform us. If we are unwilling to change we will abandon prayer as a noticeable characteristic of our lives.

(from Celebration of Discipline, Hodder & Stoughton, 1999. Used by permission.)

So true prayer is a gift from God which allows him to be God. It's much more than a one-way conversation!

What makes prayer effective?

When Jesus' disciples requested, 'Lord, teach us to pray' (Luke 11:1), he responded to their request with what we call 'the Lord's Prayer' (Matthew 6:9-13; Luke 11:2-4). This prayer shows what prayer is really all about. It is more accurately the 'disciples' prayer', a model for followers of Jesus to use rather than a prayer for Jesus himself to pray. Note these key features of it:

- There's a dynamic of closeness and distance, as it recognises that disciples can have intimacy with God at the same time as they recognise him as ruler.

- It recognises God's excitingly different values and priorities for his creation – and humans especially. The challenge for disciples of Christ is to understand and seek to show these in a sceptical, hardened world.

- It assumes that God is able to provide impressive resources to those in his realm who recognise their weakness and need of his sponsorship.

Notice the ingredients Jesus included in this model prayer for disciples together:

Recognises who God is (Father and King) ↦ humility and praise

Our Father in heaven,

An inclusive prayer for disciples together. 'Our (not just my) Father'

   help us to honour your name.

Come and set up your kingdom,

The big picture ↦ perspective on our lives

   so that everyone on earth will obey you,

      as you are obeyed in heaven.

recognises who we are ↦ trusting God to provide for our physical needs ...and ↦ acknowledging our failures

Give us our food for today.

Forgive us for doing wrong,

      as we forgive others.

Keep us from being tempted

Recognises spiritual realities in our world ↦ requesting God to protect us... and to meet our spiritual needs

      and protect us from evil.

Matthew 6:9-13 (CEV)

Another simple framework to help you remember key elements for effective prayer is this:

5 A's

Approach: prepare to meet God and be still in his presence.

Acknowledge: recognise who God is, his character and personal qualities.

Appreciate: express gratitude for God's goodness.

Admit: confess our failures and sin to God, asking his forgiveness.

Ask: make our requests to God for ourselves and others.

Why are Small Groups important?

Christian small groups come in 'all shapes and sizes', but regardless of their physical make-up, they all have remarkable potential to be used by Jesus to build his body, the church.

Small groups as partnership with God

Throughout history small groups have been significant building blocks for God's kingdom and his church.

- In the Old Testament, the primary Israelite institution for spiritual growth was the extended household group, essentially a 'small group' where quality relationships existed. Here values and attitudes were modelled, and both formal and informal life-settings enabled whole-of-life change in the members.

- Jesus' key strategy for the expansion and continuation of his ministry was a 'small learning community' comprised of those he called to be his disciple-companions. His concept of 'apprenticeship-in-faith' – what we call discipleship – worked best in the interactions of a small group. The disciples and Jesus spent time together, laughing, learning, crying, serving, suffering and worshipping. Through all that, they discovered the priorities and values, behaviours and attitudes that reflect life in God's special community. Growing in God was a communal activity for them.

- The basic unit of the early Christian churches in the New Testament was the *oikos*, the extended household, a significant social unit in Graeco-Roman society. Family members spanning all ages, servants, even business associates were all part of the *oikos*. Its size and composition provided the environment for the members together to fulfil the task of 'being church'. In this setting, they were able to best show the distinctive quality of their life. This is expressed in the remarkable range of 'one another's in the New Testament letters. Believers are instructed to love... care for... serve... teach... encourage... employ the gifts given by God, and so on, all for the benefit of one another.

- Small groups have frequently been significant during times of notable church growth. Examples that spring to mind are:

  ... in the first churches, small travelling teams of men and women led by people like Paul and Barnabas, and resourced by the Holy Spirit, travelled throughout the Roman Empire to evangelise and nurture the numerous new Christians.

  ... in the later Middle Ages, Anabaptist mission-minded small groups – despite a great deal of persecution – were instrumental in taking the Gospel into various parts of Europe.

... in the 18th century, John Wesley's class meetings, out of which the Methodist movement blossomed, contributed to the 'awakening' which was to have widespread influence.

... in the 20th century, amazing spiritual energy was released by the base ecclesial communities in South American countries and house-churches in China.

... and most recently, the cell church movement and the Alpha programme have had world-wide impact.

Recognising God's values in Christian small groups

What is it about small groups that make them an effective part of God's strategy for his kingdom? Think about these important biblical values which may be recognised in small groups.

- God is essentially a small group. The Trinity – God as Father, Son, and Holy Spirit – is a community of three, in one!
- Community is God's design for well-rounded human growth. We can't grow mature as loners or as anonymous members of the crowd. We grow as whole persons in the setting of community: family, friends, church. Spiritually, we need to be accountable to others for our growth, and we need to take some responsibility for the growth of other Christians.
- God's purposes are for the church as a community. The New Testament challenges Christians to live as the people of God, the body of Christ, the fellowship (*koinonia*) of the Holy Spirit. These are all expressions of meaningful community, not of individuals or faceless crowds.

Partnership dynamics of small groups

Churches vary, but there are a number of advantages in having a small group structure for the way we 'do church'. One missions-focused writer, Howard Snyder has suggested these potential advantages of small groups over larger gatherings of Christians:

At their best, small groups may be:

- flexible, relatively easily able to change how they operate or to modify their objectives;
- mobile, not bound to particular buildings or locations;

- inclusive, able to draw in newcomers easily and in a relaxed way;
- personal, of a size in which people can relate to face-to-face;
- able to take risks, and to live on the edge of adventure; and
- run with a minimum of professional leadership.

(Adapted from Howard Snyder, The Problem of Wineskins. IVP, 1977, pp. 140-142.)

Where have such advantages been modelled? Look again at the examples above of small groups in Christian history. Such features contributed to the significant impact of those groups, showing that small groups are a particularly potent structure for Christians to partner with God, expressing his kingdom in the world he created.

The potential when prayer and small groups are integrated

Consider what can be demonstrated and achieved by both effective prayer and effective Christian small groups, together:

1. Both prayer and small groups are an expression of community – between God and people, and between people themselves. Small groups and prayer both witness to the unseen but nevertheless real *koinonia* (fellowship) of God's kingdom.

2. Both prayer and small groups are places where Christians may sense that they are 'at home.' Both are places where warm hospitality may be experienced, one's identity affirmed and strengthened, and loving correction given and received graciously.

3. Both prayer and small groups provide a setting to allow God to work at re-forming us to reflect his life. This reshaping, also termed spiritual growth or transformation, has been defined in this way:

   [Spiritual growth is] a process of becoming more integrated, more whole. It is a process of bringing into harmony with one another my mind (intellectual belief), my heart (emotions), my will (choices), and my actions (expressed through my physical body) ... the goal of such integration of mind, emotions, will and action is a greater freedom to love and serve God in his world

and in others...

Sheila Pritchard

(from, Spiritual Growth, Spiritual Hunger, Reality, Dec. 1989-Jan. 1990.Used by permission. Reality is New Zealand's Christian magazine, available by subscription from their website www.reality.org.nz.)

Prayer and small group interaction together enhance this integration.

4. God helps us become fully-formed disciples through both prayer and small groups. Change may be in any of these areas:

Thinking
Understanding our faith as Christians, and how this affects every aspect of our life.

Emotions
The range and quality of the feelings we have towards God, ourselves, other people and God's creation.

Tendencies
Practical demonstrations of God's Spirit at work more and more consistently in us (e.g. 'the fruit of the Holy Spirit' – Galatians 5:22-23).

Self-esteem
Accepting ourselves fully because we know we are accepted by God.

Relationships
Copying the example of Jesus in our desire and ability to enter into caring relationships, enabling us to 'love our neighbours as we love our [God-accepted] selves' (Luke 10:27).

Development of special gifts
Recognising and using the special spiritual gift(s) which God has given us to enable the Church to fulfil its mission.

Responsibility
Accepting the responsibilities of membership of God's 'kingdom-community' - by becoming involved in service (ministry) both within the Church and in wider society.

(Adapted from B. V. Hill, The Greening of Christian Education, Lancer Books, 1985, pp. 110-112.)

As we pray that God will change us to reflect his glory (2 Corinthians 3:18), and as we open ourselves up to one another in small groups, any – and all – of these areas may be impacted.

5. Careful and sensitive listening is important in both prayer and small groups. In prayer, this is especially so towards God, while in small groups it is to other members as well as to God. Developing our listening skills in either area will help in the other.

6. Both prayer and small groups are essentially mission-minded, as they can help us sense and respond to God's heartbeat for his world. This concern may be fanned into flame both when we pray and when we participate in small groups.

Prayer and small groups, each in their own right, provide significant potential for Christians to grow. So, something quite special for God may happen when they are creatively and sensitively integrated!

Is this your experience of prayer in small groups?

No? *Then use ideas from Chapter 3 to get started.*

Yes? *Check out some of the different ways you might be able to enhance the good things already happening, by using some of the ideas in Chapters 4 and 5.*

helping groups to pray aloud
chapterthree

Despite your best efforts, you may find that prayer in your small group just isn't sparking. This calls for a number of challenges to be recognised and dealt with.

Wang said 'Lord' a lot. I'd better do the same

Ben quoted 4 verses; what verse can I use?

Joan prayed for 2 minutes... I'll try for 3!

Bless all the sick people, Lord...

Lord, we pray for the universe...

There's nothing left for me to pray for!

People struggle to pray aloud in small groups for two main reasons:

1. Fear of 'getting it wrong'

Some people wonder what the 'right' words and format are, what to pray for, and in what detail. They are afraid they will embarrass themselves because they aren't confident that they can 'get it right'. Long-time group members often seem to be able to make their prayer sound really 'spiritual', and this may scare off others.

2. A wrong perception of group prayer

Commonly, prayer in small groups is like people queuing to use a telephone. It is as if one person talks to God, and then hands over the telephone to the next person to speak. The result is a series of monologues, rather than a conversation. So no wonder that when one member prays at length and covers a wide range of topics, it is very difficult for the other participants to stay alert and focused.

Group prayer doesn't need to be like this! There *is* a place for one member to pray on behalf of the whole group, or to pray at some length. But prayer in a small group can be much like a normal conversation with one another and with God. This conversation together with God can be marked by usual patterns of speech, some spontaneity, and the shaping of a united and integrated prayer. It also demonstrates that God wants people to 'be themselves' rather than trying to impress.

Steps to effective group prayer

Effective group prayer seldom comes naturally. The steps outlined in this chapter are carefully graded to take beginners in group prayer to a position where they are comfortable in a group prayer situation. They are designed to move members through the pitfalls outlined to a much more genuine group experience.

Each step is structured in a similar way:

1. a reason for the step, based on a difficulty which people have in group prayer;
2. a coaching tip for the step; and

3. an action plan for members to acquire the appropriate skill.

Skills need to be acquired, but remember that it is the Spirit of the living Christ who is our ultimate teacher. So as you coach people in methods, remember that you partner with God to enable group members to listen and respond to his Spirit.

Your group is unique

- If your group is already on the way to effective prayer, start with the step which will help you move on to the next stage.

- If all members are comfortable praying aloud, use these steps to remind them of some of the basic principles for meaningful prayer, and to encourage them to revise their group prayer skills.

- If your group members have mixed experiences of praying aloud, you may need to quietly request the more experienced pray-ers to be disciplined in practicing these steps, for the sake of the less experienced members.

Step o : Prepare to pray

Prayer for beginners

The concept of prayer may be quite new to some, especially if they have only recently become Christians or started attending a Christian group. Before starting out on the adventure of group prayer you may need to help these people understand what prayer is. Ideas in Chapter 2 are useful for this.

Coping with distractions

Assure members also that it is quite normal to be distracted when we pray, whether alone or in a group. But these distractions can be minimised. Raise and comment on some of these more common strategies for coping with distraction in prayer:

- Some of the distractions can be readily avoided. Remind members to turn off their mobiles and pagers.

- When we become conscious of external noise while praying, we can quietly acknowledge it to God, and seek to re-focus on our prayer.

- Distractions may be caused by physical factors. Check the room temperature and ventilation. Change your posture or chair if you are seated on furniture which is so comfortable it induces sleep, or on which you just can't get comfortable.
- Our thoughts sometimes wander, or we daydream, especially if we are not used to being quiet. At such times recognise the distraction, apologise quietly to God, and then return to the prayer. It may be helpful to have paper or a notebook handy, and jot down tasks or ideas which come to mind. You can refer to these afterwards and then take appropriate action, whether it is to raise a matter in the group or do something once you leave the meeting. In the meantime you will be able to concentrate on prayer.
- The name or face of a person may come into our thoughts. This may be a prompt from God. Pray briefly and quietly for the person, or jot their name on a piece of paper to remind you later to contact them or plan to do something concerning them.

Step 1 : Write a prayer — say it silently

The stepping off point for praying aloud is to construct a simple prayer before praying it. This helps people decide what they want to say to God, and to start to feel relaxed speaking with him.

Coaching tip
Prayer is not for experts only! As children may talk freely with their parents, so as Christians we are to talk freely to our heavenly Father, without embarrassment or formality. Sometimes, we may want to prepare what we would like to say to God, just as we might when we have an important meeting with someone. ,

Action plan
1. Ensure that members have paper and a pen. Suggest an idea about which they could write a prayer of one or two sentences. For example, at the start of a group time, invite members to think of something since you last met that they are thankful for; or at the end of a Bible study, get them to think of an area in their life where they need to change. Group members could be invited to suggest possibilities.

2. Ask members to write down a short sentence for which you've given them the opening words. For example, '*This past week I'm thankful*

for (better communication with my daughter)'; or '*As a result of this study I think we need to* (be more open with each other)'.

3. Direct members to delete the opening words, and replace with appropriate words addressed directly to God, so '~~This past week I'm thankful for...~~ Thank you God for better communication with my daughter'; or '~~As a result of this study I think we need to...~~ Please help us, God, this week to be more open with each other'.

4. Invite members to read their completed prayer to God, in silence.

5. The leader may then conclude with a brief and relevant prayer spoken aloud, like, 'God, there's much that we've been thankful for since we last met. Thank you that you have heard our prayers. Amen'

Step 2: Write a prayer – say it aloud

Many people find praying aloud daunting and it may seem unnatural to begin with. Often those who feel like this have attended church for many years but are only recently involved in a small study or growth group. We can support these members to 'break the sound barrier' by encouraging them to pray aloud a simple prepared prayer.

Coaching tip
When we pray we don't need special words, a holy voice, or the ability to say a lot. Our aim is not to impress each other, but to speak simply with God. So it's OK to prepare what we want to express if it will prevent us being tongue-tied.

Action plan
1. Apply Action plan points 1-3 from Step 1. Of course, make the focus something relevant to the group at the time.

2. Invite members to take turns to speak their sentences aloud as prayers to God. Indicate the general direction around the group in which members may take their turn, for example, clockwise, starting with the leader. Assure members that it is OK if they choose not to pray aloud. They can indicate this by gently nudging the person next to them.

3. Members pray their prayers aloud and consecutively, until all have had the opportunity to participate.

4. The leader concludes with a brief and relevant prayer, and/or everyone says aloud together a prayer they all know, such as the Lord's Prayer, or a benediction.

Step 3: Domino prayers

Worthwhile group prayer is more than a series of individual prayers; it is one prayer constructed of the shorter prayer contributions of the group members. To create an integrated group prayer we need to listen carefully to others, so that we can build on what they have prayed. 'Domino prayers' helps members to do this.

Coaching tip

When we pray with others we can show that we are actively participating by consciously adding on to what they pray. This affirms that their contributions are important to the construction of a group prayer.

Action Plan

1. Explain that the game of dominos provides a strategy for effective praying in groups. In dominos, players try to match the dots on tiles in their hands with the dots on the end tiles on the table. Similarly, when we pray in groups, we can pray about the same topic as the person preceding us, before introducing a new topic or idea.

2. Suggest a focus for the prayer time (for example, praying for group members' needs in their workplace) and perhaps an order in which members may pray.
Note: At first it is appropriate to suggest that members pray consecutively around the group (except if anyone wishes to pass: see Action plan point 2 in Step 2 above). As people become more adept at praying this 'domino way', encourage them to pray in any order while still maintaining the discipline of consciously building on the previous person's topic. Similarly, members may contribute to the prayer more than once.

3. The leader starts by praying a short prayer (one item only).

4. Each person then prays a 'double prayer'. The first half of their prayer builds on the second idea of the prayer before and the second half introduces a new idea.

Example of a domino prayer

Leader: 'Lord, please help Peter juggle his responsibilities in his department this week as it's going to be especially busy.'

Member 1: *[Idea which builds on the previous item]* 'Yes, Lord, and particularly help Peter know how to deal with his colleagues Mike and Jane, who tend to be disruptive in the planning meetings;' // *[and adds a new idea]* '... and I'd like to ask you to be close to Mary while she is on sick leave, because I know she's feeling really bad about being away so long.'

Member 2: *[Idea which builds on the previous item]* 'We know how hard it will be for Mary to be catch up on her project deadlines, Lord, so will you please help Mei Lin and me to look for ways to take some of her work load.' // *[and adds a new idea]* And, Lord, we still need to find a suitable date for our office Christian fellowship retreat. Please help us to be willing to juggle some of our commitments so all of us can attend.'

... and so on.

5. The leader ends the prayer to a suitable way, or the group says a known prayer aloud together.

6. Take a few moments to debrief with the group on the domino method. Were people disciplined? Do you need to use the method several more times so that people become less self-conscious about the method, or more familiar with applying it?

Step 4: Conversational prayer

Good group prayer is like a conversation: a group of people talking together, consciously including God.

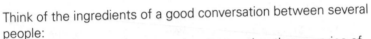

Think of the ingredients of a good conversation between several people:

- Individual contributions are quite short, rather than a series of uninterrupted and lengthy monologues.
- Participants talk more than once, in any order.
- No one exhausts everything about a topic. Instead, several people bring different ideas to aspects of each topic.
- A new topic is naturally introduced into the conversation when it is sensed enough has been talked about on the previous topic.
- Everyday language is used.
- Participants use 'I' rather than 'we', unless they know that it is appropriate to include others in what they are saying.
- Participants are not afraid of silences, seeing them as opportunities to think and reflect before speaking again.

Similar features of a good conversation can be used to enhance the quality and enjoyment of prayer in small groups too.

Coaching tip

A group can develop its corporate prayer by applying the dynamics of good conversations. By consciously building up a group prayer as a flowing conversation between several people and God, members are more likely to be actively engaged and to own the prayer as 'their group's prayer'.

Action plan

1. Highlight the features of good conversations, and explain how these can be used for group prayer. Mention also that conversational prayer is open-ended. There is no formal ending (e.g. '... in Jesus' name, Amen') at the end of each person's contribution.

2. Decide on the topic for the prayer.

3. The leader starts the prayer, and concludes it in a suitable way.

4. At an appropriate time later, discuss how this method worked. Do you need more practice at 'domino prayers' before trying conversational prayer again? How can you enhance the sense of 'conversation'?

Note: Effective conversational prayer is dependent upon members applying the principles of Steps 1, 2, and 3. If necessary, remind the group of those earlier steps. Discipline may be needed by those who are used to praying in 'monologue style'. Ask such people (privately perhaps) to consciously try to apply the principles of conversational prayer, for the sake of the group.

Step 5: A world of creativity ahead...

Once group members have practised these steps, they will have solid foundations for effective group prayer. As members naturally apply these skills, the challenges identified at the beginning of this chapter will be less intrusive and distracting.

That's the time to explore new and creative avenues for prayer. The following chapters provide a springboard for further discovery, adaptation and action in this new adventure.

variety - the spice of small group prayer life

chapterfour

Consider this smorgasbord of possibilities for praying in small groups:

with eyes open or closed

seated, standing, kneeling or prostrate

'off the cuff' (extempore) or prepared prayer

spoken aloud or silently

one person at a time or altogether aloud at the same time

spoken, chanted or sung

conversationally or one person on behalf of all

with movement or being still

How many of these have you experienced? Have you experimented with other ways of praying in your small groups? There's an amazing number of variations when such forms are combined with different elements of prayer (like the 5As). The permutations are amazing – and limited only by your creativity.

Why be creative in prayer?

1. God is a creative God

When did you last recognise the variety of God's creation around you? Or appreciate – and sigh with relief – that you are not a clone of other people?

Our God is a creative God. If we are bored when we pray in our small groups we can't blame God for being boring! Day-by-day God shows in wonderful ways that he has provided the gift of creativity for everyone. And God's creative resources can be used when we pray in small groups, too.

Of course, variety alone can't ensure a spiritual dynamic to prayer (that is the result of keeping close to God and allowing the Holy Spirit to guide the group), but praying in different ways may limit tedium and predictability. Consider the potential for increased spiritual momentum in these situations:

- A new method gives me a fresh insight, which expands my vision.
- A novel approach surprises me, and I consider a new truth which informs my own prayer.
- A different prayer style or attitude is modelled, and I adopt it in my own life as a disciple of Christ.
- I'm drawn into a way of praying that I would not normally participate in, and I'm encouraged to respond to God with aspects of my personality I seldom use.

2. God wants us to respond to him as whole people

Many of us have learned to be very good at using the analytical part of our brain when we pray. This 'left brain activity' enables us to use language, to understand concepts and to think logically. And in prayer we certainly need to engage our minds – the minds which God is renewing and transforming as part of his ongoing work in us (see 2 Corinthians 5:17, Romans 12:2).

But there is more. Jesus reminded his disciples that the greatest commandment is, 'Love the Lord your God with all your heart, with all your soul, with all your mind, and with all your strength' (Mark 12:30). God wants us to love him as *whole* persons. This means being aware of, and using, the 'right brain activity' which enhances our capacity for feeling, aesthetics, creativity and imagination.

'Whole brain prayer' helps us come to God as whole persons. Holistic expression releases the potential in us for greater spiritual maturity, so that we are more in tune with God and better able to partner with him.

With this in mind, we will look for ways to express ourselves much more in the forms of symbol, metaphor, story and poem. Through these avenues a fuller expression of ourselves as we relate to God is possible, and we are able to open ourselves more to God's response to us. Practical examples follow in this and later chapters.

3. God has made us with different personalities

There is no ideal praying personality. God has made each of us with different personalities, and this will be reflected in the ways we prefer to approach God, communicate with him, express our worship, and experience his presence and guidance. No way is right or wrong; they are merely different from each other!

Our personality influences what we feel comfortable with:

- People who tend to be inward-looking and enjoy time to themselves may appreciate opportunities for meditative prayer. But this form may be unhelpful for members who 'recharge their batteries' by being active and with others, and for whom prayer tends to be 'doing something' rather than 'being someone'.
- More disciplined members who like to have things settled and orderly will be more comfortable with structured, methodical prayers, perhaps prepared in advance. Others, who like to live more spontaneously, appreciate flexibility and variety in prayer, as much as in other things.
- Those who are energised by insights and ideas often prefer to express themselves in prayer in ways which are 'logical', expressing biblical and theological truth. Those who are energised more by relationships will often appreciate praying in a more devotional mode.

- The personality of some may lead them to prefer prayer which gives scope to their imagination. This may clash with those who need to bring understanding and awareness to their prayer.

In each of the cases above, how will your group cater for the prayer preferences of both sorts of members?

The danger of limiting the styles and patterns of prayer is that some members may feel quite comfortable, but others will struggle. These may feel themselves unnaturally squeezed into a mould that inhibits rather than liberates them to express themselves with God.

When we provide a variety of ways of praying, we provide opportunity for all group members to pray at times in harmony with their personality rather than fighting their intuitive temperament. They will find it affirming to be able to express themselves in prayer with a sense of greater freedom, and so find prayer more enjoyable. When, at other times, methods of prayer are used that they initially feel less comfortable with, they may come to appreciate the strengths and potential of such methods. Overall, the outcome can only be enriching.

Variety in the elements of prayer

On page 13, two prayer frameworks were suggested as encompassing essential elements for prayer: The Lord's Prayer and 5 A's.

Another well-known framework for prayer is **ACTS**:

Adoration: praising for who God is and what God has done.

Confession: admitting sin and failure and asking God for forgiveness.

Thanksgiving: saying 'thanks, God' for what God is doing in our lives and in the lives of others.

Supplication: praying for others and their needs, as well as our own. Let's briefly remind ourselves of the value of these prayer elements.

[A] Adoration - praising God

It is God who has taken the initiative to reach out to us. He invites us to respond to him by reaching out to him in prayer, so a good starting point for prayer is to focus on God. This is to take up the challenge which permeates so much of the Bible, and is expressed this way by the Psalmist:

> Proclaim with me the Lord's greatness; let us praise God's name together!
>
> Psalm 34:3 (GNB)

When we take time to appreciate God – to praise and enjoy God for who he is and what he has done – we are saved from much of the consumerist 'me-ism' and 'shopping list mentality' which so often marks prayer. It also remind us that our starting point as Christians should be with the God who has so graciously intervened in our lives.

If you are looking for prayer ideas for adoration, select from these methods

Altogether Prayer (p36)
Names of God (p44)
Pray Psalm 151 (p44)

and adapt these methods

Eyes-Open Prayer (p38)
God's Provision (p40)
Pray the Daily News (p47)

[C] Confession - admitting our sin and failure to God

Through the centuries Christians have discovered that as they recognise who God is and offer praise and adoration to him, so they become aware of their failings and sin. They confess these to God, and seek his forgiveness.

Confession is often deeply personal, and needs to be dealt with alone before God. But it is not solely an individual concern. The apostle James challenges Christians to 'confess your sins to one another and pray for each other so that you may be healed' (James 5:16). So in a group there is a place for prayers of confession, especially in response to discoveries about God and his standards. In this respect, group confession has a different quality about it compared to individual confession.

Sometimes it is important for a group to confess its failing to be an effective community of God's people. Examples from the Old Testament include when the Israelites refused to enter the promised land (Numbers 14:40), when they acknowledged that it was wrong to marry people from other nations (Ezra 10), and when they were aware that they had abandoned God's covenant with them (Nehemiah 9).

Today, group confession may be necessary when the group has been unwilling to respond to what God is saying to it, or over its attitude to welcoming newcomers, pursuing issues of justice and mercy, or being undisciplined in the use of time.

If you are looking for prayer ideas for confession, select from these methods

Pray Psalm 151 (p44)
Written prayers of confession (example on p 53).

and adapt these methods

Eyes-open Prayer (p38)
God's Provision (p40)
Group Concerns (p41)
Incarnational Prayer (p42)
Names of God (p44)
Pray the Daily News (p47)
Prayer Maps (p48)
Prayer Walk (p49)

See also the special note about prayer as confession on p 52

▌[T] Thanksgiving

> *You received Christ Jesus, the Master; now live him... And let*
> *your living spill over into thanksgiving.*
>   Colossians 2:6-7 (The Message)

Gratitude is a distinctive attitude of disciples of Jesus Christ. So Paul urges the Christians in Philippi, 'with thankful hearts offer up your prayers and requests to God' (Philippians 4:8, CEV). There is so much which we can appreciate, and groups will quite naturally want to express this in prayer.

If you are looking for prayer ideas for thanksgiving, select from these methods

Altogether Prayer (p36)
Answered Prayer (p34)
Eyes-open Prayer (p38)
God's Provision (p40)
Names of God (p44)
Pray Psalm 151 (p44)
Prayer Walk (p49)
Sensitive Praying for Others (p51)

and adapt these methods

Faith-Sized Requests (p39)
Group Concerns (p41)
Incarnational Prayer (p42)
Pray the Daily News (p47)
Prayer Maps (p48)

▌[S] Supplication: Praying for others' needs and our own

This is the element of prayer that Christians are most familiar with. Intercession and supplication both contain the idea of pleading to God on behalf of someone else. But intercessory prayer is not supposed to be presenting God with a shopping list of our wants, or telling God how to deal with other people. Rather, it is to invite God to intervene in their lives – and ours. We share our concerns consciously with God, secure in the certainty that God is both gracious and in control of everything, and is well able to respond to our requests:

If we learn prayer, pondering [Jesus'] example, then we will bring him our needs; we will not badger him with our proposals; we will rest in the certainty that our needs will be met in the perfect outworking of his will.

Alex Motyer

(from Jesus at Prayer. Christian Arena, 1989, p. 4. © UCCF. Used by permission)

If you are looking for prayer ideas for supplication and intercession, select from these methods

Faith-Sized Requests (p39)
Group Concerns (p41)
Incarnational Prayer (p42)
Pray Psalm 151 (p44)
Pray the Daily News (p47)
Prayer Maps (p48)
Prayer Walk (p49)
Sensitive Praying for Others (p51)

and adapt these methods

Altogether Prayer (p36)
Answered Prayer (p37)
Eyes-Open Prayer (p38)
God's Provision (p40)
Names of God (p44)

Adoration... confession... thanksgiving... supplication. Of course, we're not likely to include all these elements every time we pray, but we certainly will want to make sure they are included over a period of time.

A feast of prayer ideas

This section demonstrates some of the creative possibilities for small group prayer. Apply the ideas directly, or adapt them to another of the ACTS elements. Use your imagination and knowledge of your group to ensure these methods enhance your life together with God.

First things first!
Request group members to check that their mobiles or pagers are turned off as a matter of courtesy and an indication of priority. (In special circumstances, silent mode may be appropriate.)

Altogether Prayer   A   C   T   S

In some Christian groups it is common for everybody to pray aloud at the same time. In East Malaysia, for example, this is called *bersamasama prayer* ('altogether prayer').

This method reminds us that...
... God can hear many peoples' prayers at the same time – and he delights in his people lifting their voices together in adoration and thanksgiving. Members may not be aware of what other people are praying, but they will appreciate that they are part of a larger outpouring of praise.

Action plan
1. Explain that members can express their praise to God in their own words, aloud, at the same time. ('Altogether prayer' works best in a larger group in a reasonably confined space, so that members don't become too conscious of only the sound of their own voices.)

2. Encourage members to make their own audible response to God, and to be neither unduly self-conscious (after all, everyone is doing the same thing) nor concerned about what others are praying.

3. Suggest a focus for your time of praise, for example see 'Names of God' (p44). Allow a brief period of silence for people consciously to enter God's presence.

4. When the leader commences praying aloud, other members commence their praying.

5. The prayer time may proceed in several 'waves' of spoken prayer and ends when silence returns to the group.

Add mileage to this method

- Silence may be unhelpful when you first use this method, so don't allow the prayer time to drag on. Initially it will be wise for leaders to finish the prayer when they become aware that some of the members have finished.
- The leader may sound a bell, strike a note, or start quietly singing a song/hymn to alert members to conclude their prayer. Alternatively, before starting to pray set a timer for 1-2 minutes.
- [S] Use this method to focus intercessory prayer on particular people and concerns.
- Congregational worship lends itself particularly well to this method.
- In multi-cultural settings, encourage people to pray aloud in their preferred language.

Answered Prayer   A   C   T   S

Jesus wept for Jerusalem because '(Jerusalem) did not recognise the time of God's coming...' (Luke 19:44). When groups recognise and reflect on how God has been working in specific areas they have been praying about, thankfulness to God will arise.

This method reminds us that...

... God, like a loving parent, wants us to ask for what we need, and delights when we express our gratitude for what he does in response to our requests.

Action plan

1. Invite group members to tell how God has specifically answered their prayers or the group's earlier requests.

2. Thank God that he has been at work in these ways.

Add mileage to this method

- Keep a record of what the group is praying for, and specific requests made. Check this record from meeting to meeting, and encourage group members to see how God is at work in these areas. (Accurate records may also help the group maintain its integrity by reminding members of what they have actually prayed for, rather than taking credit for something they didn't actually pray.)
- [S] Use this method in conjunction with Group Concerns (p41).

Eyes-Open Prayer   A   C   T   S

Traditionally, Christians close their eyes when they pray. But 'closed eyes and bowed heads' has no more biblical warrant than other positions for prayer. And while closed eyes help concentration, it means we cut out images which could be used to enhance our prayer.

This method reminds us that...

... the use of our different senses – part of who we are as persons – can enliven prayers of thanksgiving, because these senses are the means by which we perceive much of what we can be grateful for. Thus our praying may become more meaningful when we focus on a visual image, and allow God to use our train of thought as we ponder it.

Action plan

1. Choose a 'prayer-focus', perhaps a symbol like a cross or communion elements, a photograph or poster, or a reminder of God's creation such as flowers, plants or other living items.

2. Allow a time of silence for members to observe the item, reflect on what they see, consider its source and usefulness, and allow God to speak through their train of thought.

3. Invite prayers of thanksgiving which arise from the responses evoked.

Add mileage to this method

- Use this method when the group has access to a visually-rich outdoor setting like a garden, seaside vantage point, or native bush.
- [A] If items of natural creation are used as the focus, encourage people to turn their prayer to adoring the creator.
- Focus on other senses also – sound, smell, touch and taste.
- Instead of providing specific objects/images, ask members to take out an everyday object they have on them. Either pass it to another person to focus on, or put it with the other items for all members to see.
- [C, S] The items/images do not need to be attractive. Unattractive images may challenge us to reflect on the presence of evil and sin in our and others' lives, and lead to confession and intercession.

- **[S]** Responses or items to pray for may be written on a large sheet of paper or whiteboard or displayed on a screen so members don't have to rely on their memories when they are praying.

Faith-Sized Requests   A   C   T   S

Chris and Rowan prayed generally for some months that their neighbour would respond to Jesus Christ. But it was when they prayed the small, practical prayer, 'Lord, please give us an opportunity to be friendly to Bob this weekend' that Chris and Rowan started to be aware that God was at work in their neighbour's life. Seeing this request honoured by God encouraged them, and gave them confidence to make further requests of God. Their faith grew in the process.

This method reminds us that...

... often we do not see results from our intercessory prayer because we fail to pray specifically for things that we would like God to do or give. God wants us to ask believing that our requests will be answered. Remember this challenge from James:

> But when you ask [God], be sure that you really expect him to answer, for a doubtful mind is as unsettled as a wave of the sea that is driven and tossed by the wind.
>
> James 1:6 (NLT)

And don't be surprised to see God stretching the 'faith boundaries' of your group as a result.

Action plan

1. Talk together about how you can pray specifically for particular people or events at a level that you could trust God to answer. Ask God's Holy Spirit for guidance.

2. Pray together.

3. Afterwards, watch for evidence of answers. Share these in the group and thank God for what he is doing.

Add mileage to this method
- Keep a record of what the group is praying. This will help you to persevere until there is evidence of God's answer (or to change your prayer if situations demand it).
- Remember that you are in partnership with the God of surprises. Be alert to outcomes different from what you anticipate.
- Encourage members to stretch their 'faith boundaries'. But be sensitive: don't push people too far or too fast.

God's Provision   A   C   T   S

A natural stepping-off point for thanksgiving prayer in a group is recognising the positive and good things provided by God for our well-being.

This method reminds us that...
... Christians are naturally grateful people. God has done so much in our lives that we will want to recognise his gracious and loving generosity to us.

Action plan
1. Encourage members to identify specific things they are thankful for, perhaps over a particular time span such as 'since we last met'.

2. Turn these items into prayer, gratefully acknowledging God as the ultimate provider.

Add mileage to this method
- Suggest a specific thanksgiving focus, for example 'in our family life', 'in our work places over the past week', 'as we have experienced God's creation'.
- [C, S] Thanksgiving may naturally follow confession and awareness of answered intercessory prayer.

Group Concerns   A   C   T   S

God invites Christians to be involved with him through prayer to transform church and society. This might include prayer for leaders, for people serving in tough situations nearby and far away, and for particular mission and ministry interests of your group and church. But often our prayer for others is general and quite vague ('Lord, bless our leaders...') because we haven't thought carefully about what to pray for.

This method reminds us that...

... to pray meaningfully is to be as informed as possible about what we are praying for. So we will need to make an effort to discover details about the people and situations for which we pray.

Action plan

1. Gather relevant information in advance on what you are committed to pray for. Appoint one member to take responsibility for contacting the people/organisations and bring current information to the group, or share the responsibility among the members of your group.

2. Keep the information in a folder along with photos, letters/emails and relevant articles. Alternatively, develop a computer database with scanned photos, emails and other material.

3. When specific people or situations are to be prayed for, review the current information with the group. It may be helpful to prepare a summary and/or update for members to take away for their ongoing personal prayer.

4. Vary the methods you use to pray in the group, for example, sometimes conversationally, sometimes members each praying for one concern.

Add mileage to this method

- Request regular prayer information, letters, news bulletins and email updates from Christian individuals, organisations and mission societies. Research information on appropriate websites.
- Ask members who have a particular interest in specific people or situations to get up-to-date information and bring it to the group.
- Cheap telephone calls and phone cards mean that, with a little planning, the group could have a real-time conversation with someone the group is about to pray for.
- Try to get a balance in how much information is given to the group. If it is too detailed, members may be overwhelmed; and if it is too brief, members will not be able to pray specifically.

- [T] Remember to include thanksgiving for the ways in which God has been responding to the group's prayers.

Incarnational Prayer   A   C   T   S

It is quite easy to pray for people 'at arms' length', but much more challenging to uphold needy people before God with passionate involvement. This is to respond to the challenge of the writer of the letter to the Hebrews:

> *Regard prisoners as if you were in prison with them. Look on victims of abuse as if what happened to them had happened to you.*
>
> Hebrews 13:3 (The Message)

This kind of prayer is likely to be very costly. When our prayer reflects God's heartache for human suffering, we may well find ourselves starting to think and feel as if we are sharing the same experience. A natural progression then is to ask 'are there ways we should live differently?'

Incarnational prayer is to allow God to speak to us about responding by doing as well as by praying. This may then have to impact on our lifestyle, priorities, and attitudes as we become part of God's answer to our prayers:

> *Whatever our calling, whatever the circumstances of our lives, we are all to be prayerful servants and serving pray-ers. It is not possible to be in the presence of the living God without being commissioned by him to active service.*
>
> Rosemary Dowsett

(from Prayer with Running Shoes, Christian Arena, 1989, p.13. © UCCF. Used by permission.)

This method reminds us that...

... Christians are called to follow the example of Jesus Christ, whose service of deep compassion involved his own incarnation, 'moving into the neighbourhood' (John 1:14a, The Message). He understood what people were really experiencing, and was willing to act practically and compassionately despite the cost.

Action plan

1. Identify a specific situation (unemployment, civil wars, famines, acts of injustice) which is affecting people adversely. Newspapers, television and the Internet will provide local, national, and international ideas. The people need not be named or known personally to your group.

2. Encourage group members to imagine themselves as a person in that specific situation, for example, a parent in Africa nursing a child about to die from malnutrition, a victim of abuse, or an unemployed person unable to provide for the family. Ask questions like:

   • What might they experience?
   • How might they feel?
   • What would they do?
   • Who could they turn to?
   • What would they say to their children? to God?

3. Pray together for these people. By doing this, in a special way you are sharing their experience and their cries for help.

4. Encourage the group to ask 'what should we do?' - and be open to respond practically to God's challenge.

Add mileage to this method

• Ensure that there is follow-up to the prayer and discussion.
• Resources for making appropriate responses are readily available from a range of Christian social service, mission and development organisations.
• [C, T] As the group reflects on possible action, further prayer may result. This may be confession for failure to respond earlier to the discovered situations, an unwillingness to free up resources, or thanksgiving for positive moves.

Names of God   A   C   T   S

The Bible has an amazing range of names which describe the nature of God, Jesus the Son, and the Holy Spirit. Use these names to focus on the different aspects of God's nature.

This method reminds us that...

... it is God who calls us to himself, and he deserves our praise. As we focus on who God is, we will see our own situations and concerns in clearer perspective.

Action plan

1. Encourage group members to share the names of God (or Jesus) that come to mind, for example, Father, Provider, Creator, Wisdom. It may be helpful to list them on a board or large sheet of paper.

2. Invite members to each pray a short sentence prayers of praise or thanksgiving relating to one of the names/qualities identified ('We praise you Jesus that you are the Light of the world, helping us see God's perspectives when things are gloomy'). Alternatively, develop a group prayer, where members pray in response to things that come to mind as they think on each name/quality, before moving to another one.

Add mileage to this method

- Choose a theme, for example the qualities Jesus shows when he meets people's needs; or the ways Jesus describes himself as light of the world, good shepherd, etc.
- Ask group members to think of qualities of God/Jesus/Holy Spirit starting with a particular letter of the alphabet, for example R (rock, redeemer, restorer, reconciler ...).
- [C, S] Identify names or qualities of God which lead to confession of sin and assurance that God forgives, or which are relevant for the needs of specific people, groups and/or events you are praying for.

Pray Psalm 151   A   C   T   S

The book of Psalms in the Bible shows how the Israelites expressed themselves in prayer and song to God. The psalms reveal people praying when they experienced a wide range of emotions including joy, doubt, despair, anger, excitement, contentment, and amazement. Some of the psalms are the prayers of individuals, some are those of larger groups. They provide us with models for our own prayer.

This method reminds us that...

... the psalms don't really end at Psalm 150. We can create our own

Psalm 151,152, and so on to reflect our experience of what God is doing in and through us. The psalms in the Bible model that it is OK to express ourselves honestly to God, so the psalms we create may express praise or thanksgiving, confession or anger, pleading or quiet trust as well.

Action plan

1. Choose a focus for the psalm such as thanksgiving, an expression of confident hope or confession.

2. Prepare a template similar to the example below. (Adjust it for a group size of 3-5 people.) Photocopy one for each group member or display a copy that everyone can read.

3. Divide into smaller sub-groups, if necessary, so that groups are no larger than five people. Allocate a number 1 to 5 to each member in the sub-groups.

4. Allow members time to jot down how they would finish their particular sentences, for example, Person 2: 'When I consider *how we have grown together as a group in recent weeks*, I feel that you *have been working in us in wonderful ways*'.

5. When all members are ready, they read their Psalm aloud, together for 'All' and then according to each member's allocated number.

Add mileage to this method

- For larger groups, invite the sub-groups to pray their psalms aloud in the full group.
- Some of the psalms, for example Psalm 25, 34 and 145, are acrostic in format: the first word of each verse starts with successive letters of the Hebrew alphabet in order. (The most impressive example is Psalm 119, where there are eight verses for each letter of the Hebrew alphabet). Challenge your group to write an acrostic psalm prayer.

'Do-it-yourself' Psalm of thanksgiving

(All)   Father God, we rejoice that you are with us.

(Person 1)   When I recall ....
                          I'm amazed that you ....

(Person 2)   When I consider ....
                          I feel that you ....

(Person 3)   When I think about ....
                          It reminds me that you ....

(Person 4)   When I reflect on ....
                          I think that you ....

(All)   We know you have been close to us and have wanted
                  good things for us.
                  You really are a wonderful God!

(Person 3)   How can we respond to such a wonderful God?

(Person 1)   I want to ....

(Person 2)   And I want to ....

(Person 3)   I want to ....

(Person 4)   And I want to ....

(All)   You are a wonderful God!
                  We rejoice that you have been with us.
                  We know we can trust you for the days ahead.

                  [members' choice...] Amen – Cool! – Wow! – Hallelujah!

Pray the Daily News   A   C   T   S

God loves the praise of his people, but Christ died for the world. Often groups are so involved in their own interests – even worship – that they fail to show concern for the political, economic and social events taking place around them. Paul's challenge to Timothy is as relevant today as it was then:

> ... I ask you to pray for everyone. Ask God to help and bless them all, and tell God how thankful you are for each of them. Pray for kings and others in power... this kind of prayer is good, and it pleases God our Saviour.
>
> 1 Timothy 2:1-3 (CEV)

This method reminds us that...

... God is concerned about his world – and he has given his people the responsibility and privilege to share that concern. Praying for world affairs is one of the ways we actively demonstrate our partnership with God. It is important because

> ... even in a society which does not specifically acknowledge [Christ's] lordship, we are still concerned that his values will prevail, that human rights and human dignity be accorded to people of all races and religions, that honour be given to women and children, that justice be secured for the oppressed, that society become more just, compassionate, peaceful and free. Why? Why do we care about these things? Because Jesus is Lord of society by right, and because he cares about them.
>
> John Stott

(from The Contemporary Christian. IVP, UK, 1992, p. 95. Used by permission.)

Action plan

1. Bring several copies of a recent newspaper to the group. Distribute a page or section of news to each member.

2. Ask God to show members his perspective on the events and people being portrayed, and then allow time for people to scan their section.

3. Pray together about the insights gained.

Add mileage to this method

- Before praying, allow a brief time to identify specific ways you might pray for each situation. Keep 'faith-sized requests' in mind (see p 39)
- After praying, encourage the group to discuss a practical response or action that arises from the news they have been praying about (see Incarnational Prayer on p 42)
- Instead of using newspapers, watch a television news broadcast or Internet news items, screened either live or pre-recorded. Before viewing, invite God to show his perspective to the group. Conclude by turning observations and thoughts into prayer.

Prayer Maps   A   C   T   S

Your group may want to pray for people and events in geographical locations which you can't visit in person. Perhaps you want to focus on the schools in your vicinity, countries where the Gospel is being lived and proclaimed in the midst of hostility, or the places where Christian workers supported by your church live and serve God. Visualising the locations you are praying for enhances committed prayer.

This method reminds us that...

... we will pray more effectively as we put ourselves 'on site', in the location of our prayer focus. When we can't be present physically, visual stimuli like maps will prompt our imagination and enhance our intercession.

Action plan

1. Bring to the group a large wall-map of the area you plan to pray for, for example your city, a country, or region of the world. Alternatively, prepare an outline map on newsprint or a large sheet of paper.

2. Mark on the map the specific locations which are to be the focus of your prayer, such as the schools, or the countries where your supported Christians are living.

3. Using the map as a focus, discuss specific prayer items.

4. Pray for the different locations, encouraging members to look at the map as they do so. After each location is prayed for, by one or several members, mark it with a ✝ in a thick felt pen or with a cut-out symbol. Express gratitude to God for what he has been doing and will continue to do.

5. Members will be encouraged as they see the scope of their prayer. It will also be a reminder of areas still to be prayed for.

Add mileage to this method

- Light a candle and place it on a location as it is being prayed for, as a powerful symbol of the light of Christ in the situation. Take appropriate safety precautions, especially if you are praying under a fan or in a windy situation.

- [C] A 'reverse' alternative is to have symbols or lit candles already on the map. Members identify situations where the presence (or light) of Christ has been marred or minimised (e.g. where schools no longer have active Christian fellowships, where a Christian leader has left a small church and it has struggled to survive), and remove the symbol or blow out the candle. This can lead to confession and further intercession.

- If you have a large space available such as a church hall, concrete patio or carpark, use chalk to draw an extra large map up to 10 x 12 metres. Encourage members to physically move to a location on the map to pray.

Prayer Walk   A   C   T   S

The most common setting for group prayer is members seated together. Sometimes, moving around may be an effective stimulus to thanksgiving and/or intercessory prayer. Think of the potential in these examples:

- A group meeting in a home may move from room to room. In each room prayers of thanksgiving are offered for what happens in each room. Give thanks for the meals prepared in the kitchen, for the hospitality shown and relationships developed in the living area and for the restful sleep experienced in the bedroom.

- A group may move through their church facilities, and turn their observations in different locations into thanksgiving or intercession. For example in the sanctuary people may pray for those involved in preparing and leading worship, in the crèche prayer could focus on the children of the church and those who nurture them in the Christian faith, and the library and classrooms could be reminders to pray for effective equipping of the congregation for its unique ministry and mission.

- A group committed to praying for a town, suburb, or school could plan a prayer walk through that environment.

This method reminds us that...
... God is involved in all areas of our lives, including the space we live in. We can use features of that space to stimulate effective prayer.

Action plan
1. Describe to the group the route for the walk, and the time available. Allow sufficient time. Don't attempt to cover too great a distance in too short a time, or to travel too far between stops.

2. Explain the practical details of the walk. Either encourage all to participate in audible thanksgiving/intercessory prayer at each stop; or invite 1or 2 people to pray at each point. Encourage the group members to stay close together in open areas so that they can hear each other.

3. Commit the walk to God, and then proceed. At the conclusion, round off the prayer walk with a final prayer, song, or in some other appropriate way.

Add mileage to this method
- Instead of moving to pre-planned points, invite members to stop the group to pray anywhere along the way.
- Consider singing as you move between stops, or sing consecutive verses of a hymn at succeeding stops.
- [C, S] Include intercession and confession if you sense it to be appropriate .

Sensitive Praying for Others   A   C   T   S

Use a Bible concordance, a Bible software programme, or go online to www.biblegateway.com or similar to discover the amazing range of 'one another' statements in the New Testament. These statements challenge Christians to recognise the importance of journeying together as Christians. Prayer is a special means for doing this.

But a danger in some groups is that members become so involved in praying for concerns beyond their group that their own needs are neglected. So we need to ensure time is available for mutual sharing of our lives with our group – our joys, difficulties and challenges – and for this to lead into caring prayer for each other.

> *Help to carry one another's burdens, and in this way you will obey the law of Christ.*
>
> Galatians 6:2, (GNB)

This method reminds us that...

... our groups need to strike a balance between inward and outward focus. Time in the group for members to express where they are on their faith journeys builds up group members and leads to sensitive, natural prayer for each other.

Action plan

1. Either in the whole group (if it is not too large) or in subgroups of 2-3 people, invite members to talk about significant aspects, developments or concerns in their lives and networks of relationships. Members will be at different stages in their ability and willingness to be open with others, so allow all to talk at a level they are comfortable with. Encourage them to move to increasing transparency and intimacy at their own pace.

2. After people have talked about their situation, request the other members to pray in specific and caring ways for them.

3. Remind members that shared personal concerns should be kept in confidence unless the member indicates it is OK to talk with others about them.

Add mileage to this method

- People will feel more free to raise their deeper concerns as they see others willing to open up. Group leaders can set the pattern for members in this by taking the risk to share more deeply.
- Because openness develops as we build deeper relationships with others, consider how to incorporate activities for your group which enable members to get to know each other better. These could include shared meals, recreation times like 10-pin bowling, hikes,

seeing a film together, and even a retreat or weekend camp.
- If the group prays about specific items which a member is committed to deal with before the next meeting, show your care and concern by making contact with the member between meetings, and invite an update next time you meet.

A special note: Prayer as confession

A number of the methods in this chapter are readily useable for a time of confession. This prayer may be enhanced also by methods which use symbols or visual resources (p65), silence (p64), or prepared written prayers (p57 and 67).

Because sincere confession is about owning our sin and failures, it can affect us significantly at an emotional level, touching raw nerve-ends. So whatever method you use for prayer of confession in your group, take note of these points:

- Members need to own their prayers of confession. Whoever prays aloud should use 'we' only when they know that they really are speaking on behalf of the other members, or the group as a whole.

- It is helpful to talk about the areas for confession before praying, at least in terms of general categories.

- Avoid putting people in tight corners emotionally and spiritually. For example, it is quite appropriate to ask members to think about ways in which they have ignored God in their family life, and then give or perhaps ask for examples. But don't ask each person to say to the group what they will be confessing.

- Members need to be aware that group confession can result in misplaced guilt. For example, someone may pray, 'Lord, we're all really sorry some of us haven't won anyone to Christ this past year'. While this may be factual, it imposes guilt on members who are struggling to share their faith meaningfully. Again, it is best to talk through what is going to be prayed.

- Ensure prayers of confession conclude with an assurance of God's forgiveness for confessed sin such as 1 John 1:9.

An example of a corporate prayer of confession

Allow members time to reflect, individually or in the group, before praying this prayer aloud. Pause between lines to allow members to express specific details to God – either silently or aloud.

Holy God,
we confess that often we have failed
to be an obedient church.
We have not done your will;
we have broken your law;
we have rebelled against your love;
we have not loved our neighbours;
and we have not heard the cry of the needy.
Forgive us, we pray.
Free us for joyful obedience;
through Jesus Christ our Lord.

different styles
for creative prayer
chapterfive

Your group prayer can be enhanced through the use of different prayer styles. Most of these styles can be used with any of the elements of prayer outlined in chapter 4 – adoration, confession, thanksgiving and supplication. Use these styles to stimulate your creativity, and lead you to experiences of prayer that are unique to your group.

The styles outlined in this chapter are:

- 'Electronic' prayer
- Fasting and prayer
- Liturgy and published prayers
- Music and prayer
- Posture and prayer
- Praying 'in the Spirit'
- Silence and prayer
- Using our senses in prayer
- Visual prayer
- Written prayers
- Zany prayer

'Electronic' Prayer

Prayer is about developing a relationship with God, not electronic wizardry! But electronic communications are part of the lives of most of us, and may be used to help small groups develop effective prayer. Unlike the Luddites in England in the early 1800's, who resisted the advances of industrial technology because it threatened their way of life, we generally appreciate the benefits of current electronic developments. Some Christians, however, are ambivalent about this technology. On one hand, access to it provides greater awareness of what is going on around us. It's making the world a very small place. On the other hand, uncritical use of the technology and media can subtly confuse us about what is real and what is really important, in contrast to what is merely immediate or urgent. Technology's sheer invasiveness can distort our values and our priorities.

Keeping these perspectives in mind, here are some ways to use the technology in group prayer:

1. Email and the internet can be used to obtain up to date information for thanksgiving and intercession.

2. Digital photographs placed on the internet or sent as email attachments may enhance this further, by letting us see the people and situations we are praying for.

3. Videos/DVDs from mission and social concern organisations provide informative background detail for prayer.

4. With careful preparation, telephone calls or ICQ may be used during a group session to communicate in real-time with someone for whom you are praying, or who will provide information for prayer.

5. Telephone, text messaging, and emails enable group members to keep in contact with each other between meetings. Prayer items may be shared, members can pray together over the telephone, and brief written prayers may be sent as text or email.

6. Some groups have a structured telephone-based prayer chain for special prayer concerns so that all members receive a phone call within a very short period.

7. Further suggestions are given in 'Electronic Prayer Groups' on p94.

Group members will need to decide on an appropriate level of technology to use. The decision will be influenced by each member's access to the necessary equipment (computer or mobile) and their attitude towards it. Because of rapid advances in communications technology, revisit this decision once or twice a year.

Talk together about safeguards to ensure that information gathered and passed from one to another is accurate and reliable. For example, remind members that merely because something appears on the internet doesn't make it true. Agree to maintain an accepted level of confidentiality about items shared, too.

A caution: the mission which God has entrusted to his people is primarily about relationships, not technology. So take care that enthusiasm for the use of technology doesn't override sensitivity to God and his perspectives, or to members of your group. The means you use should lead to achieving your group objectives for prayer, not detract from them.

Fasting and Prayer

Fasting has been a feature of Christian spirituality through the ages and still has a place today as an avenue for effective prayer, even though some, who love their food, wish it would quietly go away. Fasting in the Bible is not dieting. It is abstaining from food for spiritual purposes, to centre on God, and his purposes and plans. The link between fasting and prayer has been expressed this way:

> In fasting we become physically weak to claim spiritual strength... In prayer our spiritual senses are sharpened to hear God. Fasting is also a sign of mourning: we identify with God's sadness, gaining a deeper revelation of his heart towards the poor and suffering.
>
> (from Target, TEAR Australia, 1995, no. 1, p. 11.)

In the Sermon on the Mount, Jesus links fasting, as an 'act of righteousness', alongside praying and giving to the needy (Matthew 6). Jesus didn't command that people fast, but he assumed that fasting was one of the ways citizens of God's kingdom would express their relationship with God and so build a more intimate relationship with him. His teaching in Matthew 6:16-18 indicates how people might fast appropriately.

The members of a group may commit themselves together to a period of fasting related to focused prayer. The prayer could be for guidance for the group, or for special concerns. These might include areas in which they sense they are neglecting the essential tasks of justice, mercy and trusting lifestyle (Micah 6:8) or specific areas of ministry or mission in their church. Or they might fast and pray for the health of certain members or other people known to the group; or for a spiritual breakthrough in some specific setting.

Fasting need not be abstaining from just food. The principle of fasting is to abstain from what tends to control us and prevent us from sensing God's perspectives. So, members may decide together to limit, for a period of time, such things as watching TV/videos, using the internet or phone, sending text messages, or spending money on non-essentials. One group fasted from the use of musical instruments in their worship for a time.

Note these practical pointers about fasting:

- Start simply and develop further as members are willing and ready. Like any discipline, it may take time to work through the novelty or difficulty of the chosen form of fasting to the place where God can work more effectively with us.

- Group members may want to be in contact with each other more frequently during the fasting period, for mutual encouragement and accountability. At least make a commitment to contact one another between meetings, whether face-to-face, by email, telephone or text message.

Liturgy and Published Prayers

A wealth of published resources is available for groups to use in their prayer. These resources cover a wide range of topics and styles of expression, and span virtually the whole of the two millennia since the church started after Jesus' resurrection. The best known collection predates that era: the Psalms in the Bible. (See chapter 6 for ways in which the prayers of the Bible may be used today).

Published prayers, because of the thought and sensitivity which the writers have put into crafting their work, may bring refreshing and challenging perspectives to our prayer. This is often the case when they are written by people with an approach to spirituality and Christian living which differs from ours.

An example of a published prayer

Lord, make me an instrument of your peace.

Where there is hatred, let me sow love;
*   where there is injury, pardon;*
*   where there is doubt, faith;*
*   where there is despair, hope;*
*   where there is darkness, light;*
*   and where there is sadness, joy.*

Divine Master, grant that I may not so much seek to be
consoled as to console;
*   to be understood as to understand;*
*   to be loved as to love.*

For it is in giving that we receive;
*   it is in pardoning that we are pardoned;*
*   and it is in dying that we are born to eternal life.*

– a prayer attributed to St. Francis of Assisi, born 1181

Some church denominations have prepared service books which contain a range of prayers for many occasions. The Anglican *Book of Common Prayer*, and the Uniting Church of Australia's *Uniting in Worship* are examples of these. The liturgies (orders of service) for Holy Communion, Baptism and special occasions, which many churches produce, also provide valuable material for groups, for example, the prayers of intercession and confession (see the example on p53).

It is useful to draw on collections of prayers from other cultures, like African, Asian, Pacific Islands, and other Christian traditions, like Celtic, Charismatic and Orthodox. A look along the shelves of any good Christian bookshop should show the range. Perhaps you can borrow books of prayers your church leaders have found helpful. Browse through them, and select what might be useable in your group. The internet is an extensive source of prayer resources too.

Written prayers may be used at various times in your meeting – to invite God's presence as you start a meeting, or as a benediction to conclude; to provide a framework for intercession, or to sum up a Bible study or discussion. They may be read aloud by one person, or by the whole group together.

A Celtic prayer to say together at the end of a small group time

God with us protecting,
The Lord with us directing,

The Spirit with us strengthening,
For ever and for evermore, Amen.

An example of a contemporary prayer

Exhausting discipleship

There are times, strong Lord,
  when discipleship is exhausting,
like clambering along a cliff face
  where toeholds are small
  and where one's fingers and arms
  cling on defiantly to the hard rock.
At such times, grant us, please, Lord,
  ledges of respite and rest,
and the faith-courage
  to get going again,
following your firm leadership.

Bruce D Prewer

(from Brief Prayers for Australians, volume 2, p. 77. Openbook Publishers (formerly Lutheran Publishing House), 1992. Used by permission.)

Music and Prayer

Prayer in a group needn't be limited to spoken words. The Bible gives numerous examples of people expressing themselves to God through songs and music. Indeed, the book of Psalms was the prayer and hymn book of the nation of Israel.

The psalmists, Paul, and church leaders through the years have all been well aware of the amazing effect music can have on us. Music is what Leo Tolstoy described as 'the shorthand of emotion'. It is well-known that rhythm, melody and harmony combined can make a powerful impact on people for psychological, emotional and spiritual health and well-being.

Music is a gift from God to help us express ourselves to him even in prayer. So we can respond to Paul's challenge to the Christians in Colossae to 'sing psalms, hymns and sacred songs; sing to God with thanksgiving in your hearts...' (Colossians 3:16, GNB)

Use existing hymns and songs

There is an incredibly rich reservoir of hymns and songs available for prayer in small groups. They are in published hymnbooks and song collections, and on the internet. They are available as CDs and downloadable files. Favourites include traditional, well-loved hymns of the Christian faith as well as more contemporary expressions of the faith from composers like Graham Kendrick, Geoff Bullock, and others whose songs speak into our situation in a special way.

- Many of the hymns and songs sung in worship are in the form of a prayer – addressing God directly. Sing suitable ones at various points in your group's time together. The repetition of the short spiritual songs of the Taizé community (www.taize.fr) lend themselves especially well to meditation and reflection.
- Members might listen to one of the group sing a song or hymn as a prayer, accompanied or *a cappella*, and quietly make the words their own.
- Listen together to a recorded song, allowing it to become the prayer of the group members. Copies of the lyrics for members may enhance this approach.
- If your church uses a hymnbook, recognise this as a prayer resource in similar ways to those already outlined.
- Allow the folk hymns and spiritual songs of cultures other than your own to bring fresh insights to your prayer.

How to select appropriate hymns and songs

This TRIM test may help you identify worthwhile music for your group.

Theology/Teaching
Are the thoughts expressed in the words really true? Do they clearly reflect Christian insights?

Relevance
Are the words relevant to your group?
Do the ideas/attitudes expressed reflect the experience of your group members?

Interest
Are the words and music attractive and memorable to your group?
Is singing it enjoyable?

Meaning
Do the concepts make sense to your group members?

Using this test, you will be able to put songs into one of four categories:

1. Store-aways (high quality words and music, including the great traditional hymns, which you draw on often);
2. Take-aways (substantial music, 'evergreens' worth singing);
3. Throw-aways (temporary material suitable for an occasion or period of time, including specially-composed offerings); and
4. Stay-aways (to be forgotten as soon as possible, though graciously, because they are bland or trite, and fit so few of the criteria).

(Categories identified by Dr Guy Jansen, Servant Songs, Albatross, 1987. Used by permission.)

Compose your own prayer-songs
Use the creativity of group members to 'sing a new song to the Lord' in prayer (Psalm 33:3, 96:1, 98:1, 144:9, 149:1).

- Encourage group members to write their own lyrics of response to God, and set them to original music. These could be for any category of prayer – praise, thanksgiving, confession, or intercession.
- As a response to a Bible study or time of thinking through a specific issue, ask members – individually or with one or two others – to

write a verse that can be sung as a prayer to a well-known simple song or hymn tune. Re-assure members that precise rhyming is not critical.
- Possible and straightforward verse structures include
  - four lines with 8-8-8-8 syllables (as in 'When I survey the wondrous cross'); and
  - four lines with 8-6-8-6 syllables (as in 'Amazing grace')

Music for reflection
Thoughtfully-selected instrumental music, both classical and contemporary, may be used to enhance prayer. It may be 'live' (for example played by a member on guitar or woodwind instrument) or a track from a pre-recorded CD.

- Play music to create a suitable atmosphere for prayer, as the group consciously seeks to allow God to be present. This can encourage members to quieten themselves after rushing to the group, help them relax, put to one side many of the things on their minds, and focus on God.
- Some people appreciate instrumental music playing quietly in the background while they are praying. But for some this may be more distracting than helpful, particularly if the melody has recognisable lyrics not associated with the focus of the prayer.

Posture and Prayer

Body posture can significantly enhance prayer experiences. Think, for example, of ways people use their arms and hands when they pray. Some people find it meaningful to raise their hands to God while they are praising him; or cup their hands as a sign of being open to receiving Christ's love. The tax collector in Jesus' parable beat on his breast as a sign of his anguish and sorrow for his sin (Luke 18:13).

Invite group members to use different physical postures during prayer. Kneeling for prayer is commonly mentioned in the Bible, but standing and lying prostrate (face down) on the floor are mentioned in the Bible too. Experiment to discover what is helpful for the different components and styles of prayer. And don't give up on a posture until you have tried it several times, so that you move beyond the novelty or distraction of it. Intentionally changing body position may prevent members in comfortable seats from dozing off, too!

A group may express its unity in prayer by inviting members to hold hands while they pray, seated or standing in circle. When individual members are being prayed for, invite other members to physically encircle them. Members may like to lay their hands on the head or shoulders of the person. This says, in effect, 'May the love and power of God flow through me to you.'

'Praying in the Spirit'

Prayer in small groups will usually be in the normal language of the members. Sometimes, however, members may want to use a special 'prayer language' that God has gifted them with through the Holy Spirit. This language is not learnt, and is a language of the spirit rather than the mind. Those who use such languages say that it enables them to experience a greater liberty to praise God from the depths of their being, or to help them pray on behalf of someone or something that they don't know how to pray for.

As with all special spiritual gifts from God, not everyone will receive this (Romans 12:6) and people who do are no more spiritual because they have it than those who haven't received it. Furthermore, such gifts are not given to people primarily for their personal pleasure, but rather to build up the Church, as the Body of Christ, and enable it to fulfil its mission.

It is important to exercise this gift carefully in a group situation. When used privately, this 'gift of tongues' doesn't need to be interpreted. But when used in a more public situation, we would expect God to give someone else the ability to interpret the message given, so that everyone might benefit (see 1 Corinthians 14).

In group prayer, it is important that all members feel reasonably comfortable, included, and free to contribute. So, if one or more members want to 'pray in the Spirit', it is important for the matter to be raised sensitively and frankly in the group. Similarly, if a group has been praying and God's Spirit seems to have moved in a spontaneous and unexpected way, it may be desirable afterwards to discuss the impact of that on the group. It is wonderful to allow God's Spirit free rein to work in and through the prayer of the group, but not at the expense of unhealthy exclusiveness or alienation by members. If necessary, check your practice against Paul's challenge:

Be completely humble and gentle; be patient, bearing with one another in love. Make every effort to keep the unity of the Spirit through the bond of peace.
Ephesians 4:2-3, (NIV)

Silence and Prayer

Stop reading for a moment, close your eyes, and listen to all the sounds around you...

Our world can be very noisy, and silence is a hard-won luxury. Silence is also something that frightens many people – including Christians.

But silence need not be emptiness, merely the absence of sound. Wonder at the psalmist's challenge: 'Be silent, and know that I am God!' (Psalm 46:10, NLT). Silence during prayer can be very full and satisfyingly rich. James Houston has suggested that 'perhaps 90% of our prayer life should be silence'. It will be a challenge to most of us to pray in silence for even a small proportion of that time.

Silence may be used to good effect in group prayer when:

• It provides time for members to meditate on God and his attributes, before turning their meditations into spoken prayer.

• It allows members to prepare mentally and spiritually for their contribution to the group's prayer.

• It gives space for members to make their own deeply personal, intimate response to God – in confession, thanksgiving, and/or intercession. These times may be structured in the form of 'bidding prayers', in which the leader suggests topics for members to focus on. ('Let's now quietly ask God to show us the areas in which we need to know forgiveness'; or 'Let's commit to God those family members who are especially in our thoughts right now.')

• Following a Bible study or within a time of celebration, it allows time for God to speak to the group. This will demonstrate practically that prayer really is a dialogue, rather than one-way communication.

- Sometimes – for example when we are deeply distressed, like Job's friends (Job 2:13) – we simply may not know what to pray. The most effective prayer then is silence. The situation may be an awareness of poverty, serious illness, or disaster. On such occasions 'when we don't know what to pray for, the Spirit prays for us in ways that cannot be put into words. All of our thoughts are known to God. He can understand what is in the mind of the Spirit, as the Spirit prays for God's people' (Romans 8:26-27, CEV).

Using our Senses in Prayer

Examples have been given of how to use hearing and sight to enhance group prayer (see, for example, music, p59 and physical objects, p38). Be alert also to ways of using other senses, like touch, taste and smell, to stimulate prayer.

This is not a new idea. The Bible abounds with examples of symbols and images designed to provoke the human senses and enhance prayer. For example, the Israelites were helped to respond to God with unleavened bread, the pillar of cloud and fire, stone mounds, the items for sacrifices, incense, and the furnishings of the tabernacle and temple. Jesus used bread and wine and foot-washing.

When we use our senses, our imagination is strengthened. Imagination is our ability to use mental images to help us consider and describe what is real, but perhaps not visible, and to assist us to turn ideas into practical action. This is especially important as we try to appreciate better who God is, and his perspective for us and his world. The power of imagination for Christians is seen in this comment:

> Under God, our imaginations – when devoted to his glory and informed by scripture – can open up the riches of his grace in ways not possible through the use of reason alone. Imagination and faith go hand in hand. And, as in so many things, children can show us the way.
>
> Francis Bridger

(from Children Finding Faith, Scripture Union, 2000, p. 54.)

Effective building of relationships with others involves using our different senses. Prayer is about communion with God, and we do that best when we come to him as whole people, with mind and emotions informed by our senses. As in worship, the use of sight and smell, touch and taste in group prayer may raise our awareness and heighten our sensitivity to God in a way which the spoken word can't do effectively by itself. Our senses are there to help us 'hear' God as fully as possible, and to discover that he might be 'saying' much more than we usually expect.

Group prayer ideas to engage the senses

Visual
- Candles may represent Jesus as the light of the world, or the light of the gospel in dark places.
- Praying hands could be a reminder of the mystery of prayer or our attitude towards God.
- Objects from creation, like flowers, stones and animals, may lead to thanksgiving and wonder, or remind members about qualities they possess or would like God to develop in them.
- Photographs will remind members of the people or events they are interceding for.

Taste
- Taste small amounts of sugar, salt, or lemon juice before praying for what is sweet, sour, or bitter in God's world. Or use the tastes as a reminder of aspects of what Jesus Christ has done for humanity.
- Slowly taste bread and wine or juice while praying quietly during an act of communion.

Smell
- Incense or perfume sprayed in a room may provide a richer experience for a group consciously inviting God to be present, and lead to adoration.
- Unpleasant smells (in containers with lids that can be lifted a little for members to sniff) may stimulate prayer for less attractive or ugly aspects of life, and the world around us.

Touch
- A tuft of natural wool for members to twist through their fingers could precede a prayer response to Jesus as a caring shepherd.
- The texture of a large and perhaps rusty nail held by each member may be used to evoke prayer about what it meant for Jesus to endure excruciating agony on the cross.

A combination of senses may be used to contribute to the overall impact. For example, combine touch with smell or taste, or visual stimulus with smell. Excellent resources with further examples of this are *Multi-Sensory Prayer* and *Multi-Sensory Church*, see Appendix 1: Resources .

Visual Prayers

A group may further develop the non-verbal component of life by inviting members to draw a prayer. While this may involve more preparation than normal, it is well worth attempting in order to help participants use areas of their personalities that are often suppressed.

- Make available paper, paints and brushes, crayons or coloured pencils. Suggest a theme, or use this as a response to a Bible study or discussion, and encourage members to paint or draw their own prayer response. Allow plenty of time for this – probably at least ten minutes. Emphasise that it is not a competition for the best art work! At the conclusion, allow time for members to look prayerfully at how each person has 'prayed' through their art creation.

- Alternatives to freehand art, or to complement it, are to provide pictures from magazines and newspapers and glue, and get people to create a 'prayer montage'; or provide a range of different materials for the creation of a 'prayer collage'..

- Draw a group prayer. Place a large sheet of newsprint and coloured felt pens (or paints and brushes) in the middle of a group of 3-4 people. Suggest a topic for prayer, e.g. 'God who provides for us', or 'journeying on with Jesus'. Invite people to reflect and then draw on the paper to create a visual group prayer. Members add lines, shapes, symbols and colour to build on each another's contributions. When it seems that the drawing is 'complete' or an agreed time is up, members may end with brief spoken prayers.

A variation on these methods is to play a song or hymn and encourage members to draw a prayer – either individually or in small groups – as a response to the music and lyrics while they listen to it.

praying**together**

Written Prayers

Sometimes a group will want to plan its prayer carefully by encouraging members to write the prayers before they are spoken aloud. This may be helpful when reticent members need to feel more comfortable with praying aloud; or simply to ensure a less rushed response to God.

- Invite members to write down their thoughts in the form of a prayer, so you end up with as many prayers as there are members. These written prayers can be read aloud in turn by their creators. Encourage members to indicate their agreement verbally with the prayer(s) while it is being prayed, and have a united 'Amen' (or similar) at the conclusion.

- One or two members may compose a corporate prayer based on ideas drawn from the group, which one person then prays aloud. Alternatively, sub-groups of 2-3 people can write prayers which focus on one aspect of the topic or issue. If the prayer(s) are written large enough for all to see (for example on newsprint, white board, or computer) the whole group could then pray it (them) aloud together.

Poetry and prayer

Written prayers may be in the form of poems, either rhyming or free-flowing (see 'Compose your own prayer-songs' on p 61) . Poems have potential to be particularly powerful for prayer because of the way they encourage us to 'think in pictures and images' and so relate to our experience and feelings rather than just our thoughts. This will enable us to respond much more as total persons.

Two poetry forms to experiment with for prayer are the *haiku* and *cinquain*.

- Haiku verses (originally from Japan) traditionally consist of 17 syllables, arranged in three lines of 5, 7 and 5 syllables. But there are now lots of variations – search the internet to discover the possibilities.
- A cinquain is a 'diamond-shaped' verse, with five lines consisting of 1, 2, 3, 5, and 1 word respectively.

Line 1: one word to
name/address the subject

God

Line 2: two words to
describe the subject

Creator, Shaper

Line 3: three action words
about the subject

forming, moulding, perfecting

Line 4: a four or five word
phrase describing the subject

**Imaginative mind energising human
potential**

Line 5: one word that
sums up the subject

Amazing!

Zany Prayer

Prayer can be enlivened by thinking 'out of the box' occasionally, in
slightly unorthodox and fun – but still meaningful – ways.

Prayer darts Ask group members to write a specific personal prayer
item on a sheet of paper about A4 size. Instruct them to fold it into
a dart (paper glider). When the leader gives the word, all members
launch their darts into the air ('offering the items to God'), and pick up
someone else's. Re-launch the darts several times to ensure they are
truly mixed up. Each member then retrieves one dart and prays for the
item and person represented by the dart.

Prayer balloons Invite each person to write a prayer item on a small
slip of paper. Items may be anonymous or named. Fold the slip tightly
and place it in an uninflated balloon, which is then inflated and tied.
All the balloons are tossed around for a short time before members
retrieve one each. They burst it, recover the slip, and pray for the item
individually or conversationally with others.

Prayer web This prayer activity is particularly meaningful when a
group wishes to emphasise its unity. Bring to the group a ball of string.
Members need to be seated more or less in a circle. Decide on a focus
for prayer. The leader holds the end of the ball of string (firmly), prays
a sentence on the agreed focus , and then throws the ball of string

praying**together**

to another member. In turn, members pray, holding the string, then throwing the ball of string on to the next person. When all members have contributed, a string web is formed. Conclude the prayer by recognising with God what the web symbolises for the group. Invite people who wish to pass to simply hold the string when it comes to them and throw the ball onto someone else.

mɛm® prayer Buy a pack of multi-coloured small sweets. Use the different colours of the sweets to represent a particular prayer focus. People each take one sweet from the packet (together or in turn), and then pray according to a displayed colour code.

For example, a missions-focused group praying for the schools in their town might use this colour code:

Red = thanksgiving for what God is doing in the schools.
Blue = the school administration.
Yellow = challenges facing the Christian students.
Brown = the teachers.
Green = the Christian fellowship groups in the schools.

integrating the bible with prayer

chaptersix

God communicates with people in a variety of ways. Creation, circumstances, and other people bring his message to us. It is interesting that the New Testament speaks of Jesus as 'the Word of God' (John 1 and Revelation 19:13), but doesn't specifically describe the Scriptures in the same way. Jesus is, uniquely, the living Word of God, and nothing should be said of the Bible to take that unique place from him.

But the Bible often speaks of God's communication to men and women through the Scriptures as his word. Paul, writing to Timothy, reminds us of their value:

> *Every part of Scripture is God-breathed and useful one way or another – showing us truth, exposing our rebellion, correcting our mistakes, training us to live God's way. Through the Word we are put together and shaped up for the tasks God has for us.*
> 2 Timothy 3:16-17 (The Message)

For Christians, the Bible as 'God's special book' is a key to growth. It is there to be read, studied, meditated on, and its principles and insights applied in daily living – however challenging and hard-hitting that may be. There is a wide assortment of ways in which the Bible can be used to help us re-calibrate our lives:

> *Through the Bible, God may want to disturb us, comfort us, humble us, make us less sinful, encourage us, give us hope, guide our decisions, make us squeal with delight or gasp with wonder, or help us to love him more in another way. God's word can change our thinking, feelings, actions and wills. To let God*

*change us in any of these ways, through what we read or hear
in the Bible, is to recognise its authority. In the end, we are not
talking about the authority of a book, but the authority of God.*
Terry Clutterham

(from The Adventure Begins, Scripture Union,1996, p. 20.)

There are a number of strategies that will help small groups to create
a dynamic partnership between God's two most common means
of communication, the Bible and prayer. Try some of these ideas,
adopting and adapting to ensure a good fit for your group:

- Bible blessings / benedictions
- Make Bible prayers your own
- 'Mark my word'.
- Meditative prayer
- Pray the Bible
- Write a 'Bible prayer'

Bible Blessings/Benedictions

*May the grace of the Lord Jesus Christ, and the love of God,
and the fellowship of the Holy Spirit be with [us] all.*
(2 Corinthians 13:14 (NIV)

The Bible is a rich reservoir of blessings and prayers like this one,
which can be used as group members depart from a time together.
Other well-known benedictions from the Bible include Numbers 6:24-
26, Romans 15:5-6, Ephesians 3:20-21, 1 Thessalonians 5:23-24, and
Hebrews 13:20-21.

Action plan

1. Select the Bible benediction which is most appropriate for your group
   to conclude a meeting with.

2. Either one person say it aloud, or the group say it in unison or sing it.

Add variety

- Most often, people close their eyes during benedictions. But
  because they are 'good words' (the meaning of 'benediction'), said
  to participants, encourage members to look at the person saying the
  benediction (or at each other, if it is being said in unison).

- Express solidarity with each other while the benediction is said, by holding hands, standing in a circle, and/or putting arms on or around the shoulders of the persons on either side.

Make Bible Prayers Your Own

The Bible contains numerous prayers which can be used as the basis for a group's prayer.

- Many of the Psalms were used originally by God's people praying and worshipping together, in a variety of situations and expressing a wide range of emotions. Compare, for example, the feel and focus of Psalms 8, 67, 74, and 92.

- The Old Testament has numerous examples of prayers by, or on behalf of, groups of people, for example, 1 Chronicles 29:10-19 and Nehemiah 9.

- Sense the scope of Jesus' prayers for others, for example in John 17. Recall the features of the prayer Jesus taught his disciples (The Lord's Prayer, Matthew 6:9-13, Luke 11:2-4 - see p12), which Christians regularly make their own as they recite it together.

- A number of Paul's letters commence with a prayer for the letter's recipients, for example, Philippians 1:3-11, Colossians 1:3-14, Philemon 4-7.

Many of the prayers in the Bible have potential to be used by groups today. They may be used 'as is', if the ideas expressed are relevant to the group, and reflect how members want to express themselves before God; or they can be adapted to the group's more specific focus.

Action plan

1. Choose a Bible prayer that suits the occasion of the group (or use a Bible prayer that has been studied by the group).

2. Pray the passage aloud. Either one person reads it aloud for the group; or the members read it aloud together. Don't rush. Allow time for the words to make an impact.

Add variety

- Different members may read aloud sections of the prayer. However, ensure that the passage is divided up into 'sense-bytes', rather than rigid verse-by-verse divisions. Check for places where the sense flows over verse breaks.
- Instead of reciting the Lord's Prayer at its normal pace, encourage the group to take 5-10 minutes to say it. The pauses between phrases can be used for personal reflection and prayer.
- Adapt one of Paul's prayers to pray for a particular person or group of Christians. For example, using Philippians 1:9-11: 'Father God, we pray for Bee Tan and Jason, that their love for you will keep on growing and that they will fully know and understand how to make the right choices, so that they will still be pure and innocent when Christos returns. And until that day, may they allow Jesus to keep them busy doing good deeds that bring glory and praise to you...etc.'

'Mark My Word'

Mark my Word provides a framework for integrating prayer with meditation on a Bible passage. It can be used as the basis for the study of a particular passage, or as a focus for prayer following a Bible study.

In this method, members mark the Bible text with arrows pointing in three different directions. They then use the arrows they have drawn as the basis for a prayer response to what God has been communicating in the passage.

Action plan

1. Members read the selected passage quietly. As they read, they individually draw arrows in the margin of their Bibles adjacent to discoveries about God, areas of conflict, or directions for living God's way. Use this guide:

Draw this arrow...	for discoveries about...
↑	God: ... the Father/Creator; ... Jesus the Son; ... the Holy Spirit

↓	Us: ...the sort of people we are without God; ...the problems we meet when we are in conflict with God
→	Directions for living with God

Note: Leaders may want to check, before the session, that there is sufficient in the chosen passage to ensure members will be able to place some arrows. But don't expect to find examples of all three arrows in every passage. On rare occasions, as in some Old Testament passages, it may be difficult to find material for any arrow. And don't force questionable interpretation of verses for the sake of getting arrows.

2. After a period of personal meditation and marking, the group prays together, using these key words to focus the prayer.

Direction of arrow	Key words for prayer response
↑	• We give **praise** for who God is and for the things we have discovered about God in the passage. • We give **thanks** for those things the passage reminds us of, that God has done for us: for helping ... healing ... leading... correcting.
↓	• **Forgive** us for our failures. • **Strengthen** us to overcome the temptations read about. • **Protect** us from the sins described. • **Rescue** us when we are reminded of a sin not easy to overcome.
→	• **Help** us to put into practice what we have learnt. • **Lead** us in new directions discovered. • **Teach** us about what we don't understand. • **Keep** us faithfully following as God continues to lead.

Add variety

- Mark my Word lends itself especially well to the Psalms and Bible passages which have direct teaching, such as Jesus' teaching in the Gospels, and Paul's letters.
- Members may wish to share their main discoveries before praying, especially if this method is being used for a Bible study. If your reason for using this method is more meditative, however, take care to avoid becoming too study-oriented.

If members prefer not to mark their Bibles, provide a copy of the Bible passage – either photocopy the passage from a printed Bible, or download the relevant passage from an internet site like www.biblegateway.com.

Example:

> *Jesus said to his disciples: 'If you love me,* ➜ ①
> *you will do as I command. Then I will ask the*
> ② ⬆ *Father to send you the Holy Spirit who will*
> *help you and always be with you. The Spirit* ⬆ ④
> ③ ⬇ *will show you what is true. The people of this*
> *world cannot accept the Spirit, because they*
> *don't see or know him. But you know the*
> ⑤ ➜ *Spirit, who is with you and will keep on living*
> *in you.'*

John 14:15-17 (CEV)

Possible prayer responses from this passage:

 ➜ ① 'Keep us showing our love by obeying you, Lord.'

② ⬆ 'We praise you God that you have sent the Holy Spirit to help us, especially at the times we don't know how to speak your words.'

③ ⬇ 'Please forgive us, Spirit of God, for the times when we haven't accepted your direction for our group.'

↑ ④ 'Thank you God that your Spirit shows us what is true.'

⑤ → 'Please help us to be more conscious of your presence, Holy Spirit, especially when we are tempted to sin.'

Meditative Prayer

In a small group, a straightforward way of integrating the Bible and prayer is to flow from a time of Bible study into unhurried meditation followed by prayer.

Meditation here is akin to that referred to by God's words to Joshua:

> *Study this Book of the Law continually. Meditate on it day and night so you may be sure to obey all that is written in it. Only then will you succeed.*
>
> Joshua 1:8, (NLT).

In this sense, meditation is filling the mind as you dwell on God and his ways rather than emptying it; and it is active rather than passive. One writer has suggested that if reading and studying the Bible is likened to taking food into our mouth, then meditation is like chewing the food:

> *... some of God's address may be sweet and we relish its refreshing savour. Some may be bitter and we will be tempted to reject it. Some may be tough to chew and we may be tempted to set it aside. Some may be like sand in our mouth and we want only to be rid of it. In meditation we begin to discover what God is saying to us at those points of our being where we are not yet what God intends us to be. This is where the bitterness, toughness, and sandiness arise. Those points are often areas of our being where we are satisfied with the status quo, comfortable in our bondage, accustomed to our brokenness. We do not want God messing around in those areas. [Meditation] is letting God do precisely that!*
>
> M. R. Mulholland

(from Spiritual Reading of Scripture. Reprinted from Weavings: A Journal of the Christian Spiritual Life, November/December 1988, Vol. III, No. 6. © 1988 by Upper Room Ministries. Used by permission. For information about ordering Weavings, visit www.upperroom.org.)

In meditative prayer around scripture – often known as *lectio divina* (= sacred reading) – we allow God to 'mess around' with us, and change us as we encounter God personally and deeply. As we read a passage, we allow it to stir up thoughts and feelings within us, recognising in the passage our own experience, or that of people we know, and God's point of view. Then we move from analysis and thinking to responding and relationship-building with God. We express our willingness for God to work out his purposes in us, with us, and through us.

In a group this encounter through meditation will be personal, but not individualistic.

Action plan

1. After studying a Bible passage in your group, invite the members to take time to re-read the passage quietly and slowly. Suggest they pause at places they are especially drawn to, and there allow the ideas to sink in. Ask them to put to one side application, implications and conclusions. Instead, encourage an openness to God's communication by means of images and heart responses.

2. After a period of quiet individual meditation, invite members to respond to God in the group in ways they feel comfortable with. Remind the group that this is not the time for an action-oriented agenda or intercessory prayer, but rather for members to respond to their sense of God among them. They may speak from what is on their hearts (even complaining to God – as many of the Psalms do). The words may be in full sentences, or they may be just spoken names or qualities of God that arise from the passage. This meditative prayer response need not progress logically through the passage; instead, allow God's Spirit to integrate the various contributions of members.

3. When appropriate, the leader or a delegated member draws the time to a close, or, all could sing a suitable song or hymn.

A feature of effective meditative prayer is that it is unhurried, so ensure that there is ample time available. It is not a good idea to use this method if you know people will have to leave in a few minutes, or there are likely to be disruptions. (Remind people again to switch off their beeping devices.)

Pray the Bible

Passages of the Bible may be used effectively to give your group a prayer focus. 'Praying the Bible' allows the passage to determine the flow of the prayer, rather than members randomly jumping from one topic of concern to another. Any prayer element might arise from a passage – praise, thanksgiving, intercession, confession, or expressing social concern.

Action plan

1. Choose a short Bible passage that relates to a theme your group would like to focus on. At the start of a group meeting a psalm is often suitable, for example Psalm 23, 65:9-13, or selected verses from Psalms 103 or 104.

2. The leader reads the first verse or phrase of the passage, and then prays an idea relating to that phrase. Other members then pray conversationally, developing the ideas of the verse or phrase. Alternatively, members may consecutively read one phrase and pray briefly: one phrase, one spoken prayer.

3. When prayer on a particular phrase seems to be complete, someone reads out the next phrase or verse, and the process continues.

4. Conclude the prayer either when the selected passage is completed or the allotted time runs out.

An example of praying Psalm 23

(Leader) 'The LORD is my shepherd... Creator God, thank you that you care for us like a shepherd.'

(Member 1) 'You provide our food; you protect us.'

(Member 3) 'And we are so much like sheep, helpless without you. We wander away from you, but you bring us back again and again.'

(Member 2) 'I have everything I need... God, you give us everything we need, too.'

(Leader) 'Everything belongs to you – all wealth, all power and all of creation. You make sure there is no shortage of what

we really need.'

(Member 4) 'But we're sorry that often we demand things you have chosen not to give us' ... etc.

Note that a group comfortable with conversational prayer (p25) will especially benefit from this method.

Write a 'Bible Prayer'

To encourage a group's members to respond to God after a study of the passage, or as intercession for others, rewrite Bible passages in the form of a prayer.

Action plan

1. After the group has studied a Bible passage, reword it as a prayer. Use first person instead of second or third person pronouns; and directly address God/Jesus.

2. Either one person says the prayer on behalf of the group; or the members pray it aloud together. Allow time between phrases for members to appreciate what is being prayed. If you are praying it aloud together, take a short time to ensure that all know what changes are being made to the written Bible text,

Write a 'Bible Prayer' example

Imagine your group has been studying Colossians 3. The concluding prayer for the group might be like this (drawn from 3:1-4): 'We have been raised to life with you, Jesus Christ, so we want to set our hearts on what is in heaven, where you rule at God's right side. Help us to think about what is there, not about what is here on earth. For we know we've died, which means that our lives are hidden with you...'

groups with potential for creative prayer
chapterseven

Effective group prayer can happen wherever two or more people meet together. The setting may be formal or informal, planned or *ad hoc*, in a church building or a commercial office, indoors or outdoors, with a group of teenagers or senior citizens. But the central focus remains the same: the participants want to spend time with God their heavenly Father, communicating with him and sensing his purposes and direction.

This chapter highlights the possibilities for prayer in a range of common Christian small groups...

... in age-related settings
> Children
> Teenagers

... in family settings
> Families
> Married couples

... in church settings
> Church prayer meetings
> Multi-age groups
> Worshipping congregations

... in creative settings
> Special interest groups
> Electronic prayer groups

The principles and methods elsewhere in this book are readily adaptable for prayer in any small group setting. But some groups have special dynamics, and it is beneficial to be alert to these to ensure prayer that really hits the mark for the participants.

Prayer in age-related settings

Children praying together

Children have attitudes and abilities which make them natural pray-ers. For example, they often seem to have...

... an implicit and confident trust that God is listening and will 'naturally' answer prayer;

... an understanding that God is interested in simple, normal everyday affairs;

... an easiness about offering and receiving forgiveness; and

... a spontaneity which shows when they talk with God just as they do with an interested adult friend they feel safe with.

These perspectives are good building-blocks to encourage children with their peers to develop their intimacy with God in prayer. But it is important to walk the fine line of expecting neither too much nor too little from children. Realistic expectations will vary from child to child, and so knowing each child helps shape those expectations. Note these points especially:

• Encourage crisp, relevant and creative prayer. However well-intentioned children may be, they are wired with relatively short attention spans and are easily bored by what is predictable or doesn't obviously relate to them.

• Children will readily imitate what they perceive to be the 'expected' way of praying in a group: how much to pray, in what style, and what sense of reverence. Because prayer is about relationship, care needs to be taken not to legalise how it 'should be done'. And because children's use of language usually outstrips their understanding of that language, encourage – and model – straightforward everyday language.

• Avoid overusing metaphorical language. Children are developing in their ability to think, but often struggle with abstract ideas, or with figures of speech. (If you have any doubts about this, ask several primary-aged children what they understand by phrases like 'Jesus in my heart', 'God the rock of ages', and 'Don't build your house on sandy land'.)

• Children intuitively use their senses to experience their various worlds much more readily than adults, so motivate prayer with this in mind. Have posters, photos, or video-clips showing Christians serving God by sharing the gospel or advocating justice and people's rights; pass around items from nature for the children to feel and smell; share personal concerns for thanksgiving and petition; get feedback from their involvement in church projects; and so on. 'All eyes closed and all heads bowed' may prevent children being distracted, but sometimes it may inhibit meaningful prayer too.

For example, during their Sunday school time, a group of children cut pictures from magazines to show ways they could demonstrate God's love to others. At the end of the session, all the pictures were placed in the middle of the group, each child took one, and then prayed a brief sentence prayer based on their picture. Another time, after discussion the children drew a picture representing what they had learned, and were then better prepared to talk to Jesus about their discovery.

- Prepare children for prayer. Talk together about topics or a focus for prayer. Suggest guidelines, but encourage them to decide on the specifics of what to pray, and/or draw something quickly. This capitalises on the way in which children integrate imagination with the use of reason. One special situation for this to happen is on children's birthdays, when children can be invited to pray for their peers.

- Suggest simple group responses after prayer sentences. For example, children may say a sentence identifying something they appreciate, and then all respond with 'We thank you, our Father God'.

- Ensure that the children follow up on specific prayer requests. Encourage them to look and listen for God's answers, and report back to the group.

- Over time, build in the full range of different types of prayer. This will help children in two ways:

   1. They will come to realise that prayer is much more than coming to God as a generous 'Daddy in the sky' with a list of what they want – a perspective they may easily pick up from the dominant way they have heard adults pray, and reinforcing their natural penchant to ask for things.

2. A focus on thanksgiving and praise will help to dissuade children from adopting a magical or 'slot machine' approach to prayer. If their understanding of prayer (modelled or taught unwittingly by adults) has led them to pick up the belief that 'if we pray hard enough, God must do what we pray for', they will seek to manipulate God to their advantage – another natural penchant.

- Don't be afraid of silence. Children, like adults, may appreciate time to enjoy God's presence and to think about what to pray.

- Capitalise on children's enjoyment of music. A number of songs can be sung as prayers.

- Good adult models are essential if children are to develop their capacity for balanced group prayer. A value of God's kingdom is that we all have an important place in the community of God's people. Adults can model this by demonstrating that children can contribute meaningfully – to adults as well as their peers.

- Affirm children's prayers, even if they sound curious or funny. Children who take prayer seriously don't intentionally set out to be funny. It is better not to laugh if a child's prayer sounds funny, as more often than not they will not have noted the humour. Laugh with children, though, if they spontaneously identify something humorous about their prayer.

Teenagers praying together

When teenagers pray together, diverse and apparently competing inherent qualities in their make-up need to be recognised. This is especially important for those who travel with adolescents on their journey towards owning a Christian faith which is uniquely 'their faith' rather than that of their parents, other significant adults or their peers.

Teenage development is usually marked by energy, a need for variety and creativity, a sense of adventure, willingness to take risks, commitment to what they consider to be important, and participation with their peers. So adolescents may bring to their prayer a fervency which challenges adults when they are involved with them in special events or projects.

Acceptance by their peers is important, so many teenagers will be cautious about doing or saying things that are 'not cool'. This may be demonstrated by them clamming up and staying almost mute in a group for fear of making a fool of themselves. So, sensitive leaders will move slowly in stretching the comfort zones of a group of teenagers. At times they may sow ideas for the teens to pick up on in their own time and way, and all the time they will avoid putting them into corners they can't readily get out of.

Effective youth leaders will also involve teenagers in determining how they wish to express themselves in prayer. This will enhance levels of responsibility and accountability that provide a foundation for maturing discipleship – an important principle in Christian youth ministry.

With group prayer with teenagers specifically in mind, note these points:

- Teenagers often appreciate, more than adults, the intimacy of the small group experience, and so the naturalness of their group prayer will tend to be related to their seating arrangements. If they feel more comfortable and natural sitting cross-legged or sprawled out on the floor, their prayer is likely to be stilted if they are seated in chairs in rows.

- Because they tend to disdain the predictable, mundane and 'boring', teenagers will benefit from the sort of variety outlined throughout this book – consider especially using multiple senses (p65) and some of the 'zany' ideas (p69).

- Most teenagers are searching for some form of spiritual experience and the intimacy often integrated with it, such that if they don't find it in a Christian group, they are likely to look elsewhere for it. Effective prayer can provide some of that experience and intimacy, and significant adults are well-placed to provide reasonable guidelines and models for prayer. Teach the skills for praying aloud in small groups outlined in chapter 3.

- Give permission and encouragement for experimentation, so that the teenagers find a level and styles of prayer which suit their stage of development rather than becoming 'prayer clones' of Christian leaders.

- Because teens may be more willing to express their thoughts and feelings to God personally than aloud, provide opportunity for written prayers (see p67) or for them to doodle with several different coloured felt pens. State clearly beforehand whether or not the members will be expected to share their prayers with others.

- Allow teenagers' faith to be stretched in prayer but ensure that it has an earthiness about it. If there seems to be excessive piety or if prayer is unconnected to everyday life, raise the concern at an appropriate time in the group, and also as part of ongoing mentoring of the individual group members.

Prayer in families

Families praying together

Families have the potential to be effective small groups, and many of the principles and methods in this book can be adapted for times when families express their Christian faith together.

As a rule of thumb, parents/guardians need to ensure that prayer with their children is at a level of simplicity, length, vocabulary and relevance that they can cope with. The dynamics change considerably as children age, and both the quality and quantity of prayer may need to be modified as they grow older. Again, try to expect neither too much nor too little from children at each developmental stage.

Two settings especially provide scope for creative and meaningful prayer within families.

'Formal family prayer'
Many families try to establish special formal times to read the Bible and pray together to encourage a sense of family solidarity in the Christian faith. Some families endeavour to have these times daily, while others manage at most a couple of times a week.

The best way to teach prayer is by praying. Parents and other adults in a household can be particularly effective models for their children to imitate. As children see that a key element in their parents' growing relationship with God is prayer, so their own enthusiasm and excitement for prayer may be kindled. The corollary is that adults may also be encouraged in their prayer, as they hear their children pray with great trust in God.

In these more formal times, many of the ideas in this book can be used or adapted. Others can be found in the books listed on page 96.

Informal opportunities for families to pray together
Family members together in a wide variety of situations provide natural opportunities for informal prayer. Consider these possibilities:

• Mealtimes
At the beginning of meals many families say 'grace' – a simple prayer of thanksgiving for the food. Don't allow this to become predictable and stereotyped. Vary it by praying in unison or by inviting one person to say it, by speaking and singing, and by using both set graces and spontaneous expressions of thanks.

At the end of some meals turn the topics of mealtime discussion into prayer. Suggest what to focus on (adoration or confession, thanksgiving or intercession) and a method, and encourage family members to participate. Planning may enhance this time.

• 'Out and about'
'Eyes open' and brief, spontaneous prayer can take on new meaning for family members in the course of everyday life. (This is the genius of Moses' challenge in Deuteronomy 6:1-9, encouraging the Israelite adults to take responsibility in the routines of life to ensure that the requirements of God's covenant were owned by all, and picked up by the younger generations.)

Prayer opportunities may present themselves to family members, for example, while travelling, visiting parks and playgrounds, and shopping. Be alert to situations like these, even if only two of the family are involved:
* seeing a person with a disability or someone from a different culture;
* admiring an aspect of God's creation or reacting to a spoiled, dirty, or littered environment;
* getting impatient because of a delay in traffic, or in a supermarket queue;
* a crisis situation, like involvement in an accident, seeing people in an

intense argument, or an act of violence;
• when a child is fearful of a barking dog or entering a new classroom.

In such situations, it is quite appropriate to pause, and encourage a brief spoken prayer response there and then, like, 'Lord Jesus, please help that angry man to keep his temper'; or at the school gate, 'God, please help Jane as she now goes into her new class'. Look for a chance at home later to review the event and pray in greater detail.

• Evenings and bedtimes
Children appreciate a sense of routine, and may anticipate prayer with an adult at bedtime. Also encourage variety in the routine by what you pray for and how you pray together.

Good adult modelling of attitudes and practices in prayer is likely to bear significant fruit. Encourage parents to talk with others occasionally about what works and what doesn't. Likewise, arrange opportunities for parents with slightly older children to highlight necessary changes in spiritual expression in families, as children make the transitions through to young adulthood.

Couples praying together

A special 'prayer partnership' can develop between the partners in a marriage or close relationship, whether or not they are parents. But like most of the significant features in a marriage, this partnership is unlikely to happen unintentionally: it will need to be worked at. Don't assume that because both partners are growing Christians, they will be making headway in praying together.

Partners should share their expectations and fears with each other, as well as practical details. Each partner is likely to have different ideas of prayer, based on their past experiences. For example, one may like to pray in a conversational style, while the other is more comfortable with praying more formally; one may like to work through lists of names for intercessory prayer, while the other prefers to pray for people and situations more spontaneously, as they come to mind. Talk about these, and recognise that no approach is either right nor wrong. Keep in mind, however, that variety and flexibility will prevent monotony, as well as having the potential to enhance one's spirituality and personality.

Prayer in Church settings

Church prayer meetings

A common lament of many church leaders is the poor attendance at their regular congregational prayer meetings. A similar concern is raised by missions and other Christian organisations. Many non-participants reckon that a 'prayer meeting' sounds about as attractive as a plate of cold porridge or a can of lukewarm soft drink.

Leaders often cite a lack of interest in prayer for this state of affairs. But it doesn't take many visits to such meetings to discover why people are reluctant to attend. The issue is not so much that people are not interested in prayer, but rather that the events fail to be effective meetings of a group of people with each other and with God.

The Spirit of the living God longs for God's people to express their partnership with their heavenly Father in prayer. How could a local church prayer meeting or a missions prayer group enhance this?

- Don't assume that when the leader says, 'Let us pray', participants will feel comfortable praying aloud. Suggest different ways of praying as a group – and give guidelines for the methods you suggest. You may need to progress step-by-step using the plan in chapter 3, even for people who have been attending these meetings for some time. Reinforce methods by repetition over several meetings.

- Build in opportunities for meditative prayer and intercession, for listening to God as well as speaking to God, for using different senses to help participants meet God, for using the Bible as a source for prayer... and so on.

- For intercession, talk together about what could be specifically prayed for. Request someone to keep a record, and at future meetings give opportunity to review how God has responded. Ask God to show how members may be involved with those being prayed for. Enthusiasm is likely to rise as people see tangible results from their partnership with God.

- Check the group dynamics. Vary group size by sometimes praying in pairs, sometimes in groups of 4-5 people. At other times someone may pray on behalf of the whole larger group, all members may be invited to contribute short prayers, or all pray aloud together (see 'Altogether Prayer', p36).

- Be realistic about people's endurance. Even enthusiastic participants are likely to loose concentration if someone else prays uninterrupted for too long.

- People may be genuinely too busy for 'yet another church commitment'. Consider meeting less frequently (fortnightly or monthly), and in the intervening period provide specific prayer ideas and information for the church's small groups and families. Perhaps allocate prayer topics to groups or families, and ask them to suggest the specifics of what could be prayed. Then plan for an effective time of corporate prayer in which all are invited to attend and contribute.

Multi-age small groups praying

From its start, the Christian church has been an age-inclusive entity. People of all ages, from young children through to elderly adults, have a contribution they can make.

The small group structures of many churches have special potential to demonstrate the biblical principle 'all ages welcome', particularly in mutually enriching times of worship and learning.

- Once a month, families of the members of an adult small group may join together for an intergenerational program. Often these times include informal fellowship over a meal;

- Children and adults may participate together in the first 20-30 minutes of a small group meeting, before separating into age-related activities. A common theme may be explored by the different groups.

- The rationale for a group's existence may be for families together to grow in their faith, and so the whole meeting is structured for this to happen with everyone together.

Regardless of the situation, prayer can be a key element. The principles and methods for multi-aged groups praying together are those outlined in this book. If children or young people are present, pay special attention to the suggestions outlined above in 'Children Praying Together (p81) and 'Teenagers Praying Together' (p84).

There are several special challenges for effective prayer in mixed-age groups:

- Adults need to check their *attitudes* to how they expect others to pray. They can model meaningful prayer to children and young people, but they need to avoid expecting younger people to pray as mini-adults. A significant attitude for adults to show is their openness to adopt some of the qualities that children and young people bring to prayer.

- Adults need to be conscious of their *actions* in prayer. Because children and adolescents are quick to mimic adult behaviour, adults are advised to check their mannerisms and the use (often repetitive) of particular vocabulary, so as to avoid passing on habits which have little underlying spiritual significance.

- *Mutuality* is important for worthwhile multi-age activity. Members need to be open to both give to, and receive from, those of other ages in the group. Members of all ages may need to be helped to learn to respect the contribution which others bring to the group prayer. This will be enhanced naturally as variety is built into the prayer. Then, members are likely to feel comfortable with the style of prayer in the group at least some of the time; and at other times may come to appreciate other styles. The mutuality will be strengthened as the group talks together, occasionally, about the developing dynamics of the group's prayer experiences.

Worshipping congregations at prayer

Corporate worship is a central activity of God's people, and the large or small congregational setting can be used to develop and reinforce the skills and practice of group prayer.

The traditional forms of prayer in worship services are for one person 'up the front' to pray, or for the whole congregation to pray aloud written (liturgical) prayers. The Lord's Prayer is frequently recited, too.

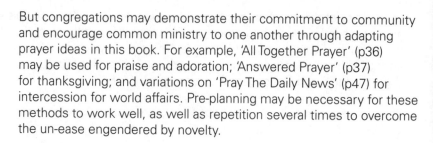

But congregations may demonstrate their commitment to community and encourage common ministry to one another through adapting prayer ideas in this book. For example, 'All Together Prayer' (p36) may be used for praise and adoration; 'Answered Prayer' (p37) for thanksgiving; and variations on 'Pray The Daily News' (p47) for intercession for world affairs. Pre-planning may be necessary for these methods to work well, as well as repetition several times to overcome the un-ease engendered by novelty.

Some congregations have discovered the potential of *ad hoc* small group prayer during their worship services. The congregation divides into random groups of 3-5 people to pray. These times may be used to pray for each another's commitment to action following the sermon, for intercession for specific concerns, or for directed thanksgiving. Creative prayer methods may enhance intergenerational worship settings.

If members of the congregation find praying aloud awkward and strange at first, give special care to ensure that participants do not feel pressured to respond. Leaders may need to start simply, with only a small deviation from the normal practice, depending on their knowledge of the members, especially in mixed-age settings. Sensitively stretch participants' comfort zones to accept and appreciate prayer styles different from those they feel most 'at home' with. Don't give up too soon: this Sunday's novel 'intrusion into our worship' may become a later Sunday's enjoyed practice.

Creative settings

Special interest groups praying

A large range of small group situations have the potential to include prayer as a significant component of their life.

You may be part of a group like one of these, or of one quite different.

Several Christians meeting for lunch at a food centre, restaurant or pub

Young mums meeting informally at a playground while their toddlers play

Two or three people commuting to or from work by train or bus

Accountability groups like Promise keepers or Renovaré

A team of Christian basketball or street soccer players before or after their game

An ad hoc group of Christians meeting to pray for a specific activity, an important decision, or for a local, national, or international event

Whatever form of small group you are in, keep these three points in mind:

- Be flexible. What is appropriate in one setting may not be helpful or workable in another. Discuss options and review regularly to keep your prayer relevant for the group.

- Encourage an appropriate level of accountability. Consider using a prayer covenant (or commitment) to set a time limit on the life of your group and have an agreed focus. Review at the end of the period, and talk about options for the next stage. For example, some members may wish to leave the group, others may be invited to join, the group may disband (especially if its task has clearly been achieved) or the group's focus may be modified. A new commitment may then be necessary.

A sample prayer covenant/commitment

With the help of God I covenant with ....
                                                          (names of other members)

to endeavour to meet .... (when? weekly/monthly?)

until .... to pray for ....
        (an agreed date)   (areas for prayer)

[or: to spend time seeking God's direction for.......................................]

Signed ....

Date ....

- Ultimately it is the Spirit of the risen Christ who enables us to pray. As we seek the Holy Spirit's help to pray effectively, so we can trust him to work out his plans through us. The resources of this book will often provide richer soil for the seeds of his purposes to take root, grow, and bear fruit.

Electronic prayer groups

Sometimes it seems that Christians in our churches can be divided into technophiles and technophobes: those who thrive on the new technology and the faint-hearted who struggle to understand it, let alone use it. If you see yourself as one of the latter, take comfort that being a maturing disciple of Jesus Christ is about a relationship rather than infatuation with technology!

But the reality is that more people will become familiar with this technology, and so it is quite appropriate to harness it where possible for Christian growth. Review 'Electronic Prayer' (p54) to see the potential and challenges of this technology.

A specialised form of small group prayer to consider is one via the electronic media – the internet and telephone. Imagine sending text messages between 3-4 people to create a 'domino' style prayer (p24);

or developing a conversational (albeit written) prayer between a group of Christian friends logged on through their computers to ICQ or a chat room. Emails can bring members living elsewhere closer to their group, with prayer concerns easily sent and received. Photos can be taken on some mobile phones and sent instantly.

Electronic prayer groups can have positive spin-offs. However, note these points as you consider developing such partnerships:

- The ability to build a level of relationshizwith someone literally anywhere in the world can be positive and significant. But as continuing news reports graphically reveal about internet meeting abuse, the honesty and integrity of participants can't be glibly assumed in non-visual interpersonal interaction. Awareness of this is necessary even among Christians.

- The ease of real-time contact (happening now, regardless of time zones) via an electronic medium may bring a sense of immediacy and urgency to prayer. Someone has had an accident, or a decision needs to be made today, and group members can be contacted instantly and urged to pray. (This communication is so fast globally that people overseas may know before others physically close to a situation.) But the buzz of the immediate can often blur concern for less urgent but more important matters.

- Quite appropriately, prayer may be encouraged as items are circulated via email or text message to members of an on-line small group. But if items are posted on a website, as information or in a blog (web log = the electronic 'diary' of a member), they need to be treated as if on an electronic noticeboard, available to anyone who cares to look. The level of confidentiality is drastically curtailed.

In the light of these points, it is best for electronic media to complement face-to-face meeting, rather than replace it. Flexibility will be necessary, depending on the people involved and wherever in the world they are located. Ensure frank discussion among the members about underlying principles and issues, and what will be appropriate to help this unique group of people move ahead on their spiritual journey.

Appendix - Resources

Prayer

Harkness, Allan, *Ready to Grow: Practical Steps to Knowing God Better*, Scripture Union, Australia, 1999. (Also available in Indonesian, Japanese and Korean editions)

Pritchard, Sheila, *The Lost Art of Meditation: Deepening your Prayer Life*, Scripture Union 2003.

Spriggs, David, *Dangerous Praying: Inspirational Ideas for Individuals and Groups*, Scripture Union, UK, 2000.

Small groups

Mallison, John, *The Small Group Leader: A Manual to Develop Vital Small Groups*, Scripture Union, UK. 1996.

Morris, Rod and Karen, *Leading Better Bible Studies: Essential Skills for Effective Small Groups*, Aquila Press, Australia. 1997.

Turner, Jennifer (ed.), *Small Groups that Catch the Wind: Using Small Groups for Community and Mission in the Local Church*, Open Books, Australia, 2000.

Personality and senses in prayer

Fowke, Ruth, *Personality and Prayer: Finding and Extending the Prayer Style that Suits your Personality*, Eagle, UK, 1997.

Mulholland, Robert, *Invitation to a Journey: A Road Map for Spiritual Formation*, IVP, USA, 1993.

Children

Merrell, Judith, *New Ideas for Creative Prayer*, Scripture Union, UK, 2001.

Merrell, Judith, *One Hundred and One Ideas for Creative Prayers*, Scripture Union, UK, 1995.

Teenagers

Carr, Elaine, *You & God: The Essential Prayer Diary*, Scripture Union, UK, 2004.

Clutterham, Terry and Wainwright, Mark, *PrayerZone: Ten Bible-Based Sessions to Energise 11-14s to Pray*, Scripture Union, UK, 1998.

Adults

Wallace, Sue, *Multi-Sensory Church*, Scripture Union, UK, 2002.

Wallace, Sue, *Multi-Sensory Prayer: Over 60 Innovative Ready-to-Use Ideas*, Scripture Union, UK, 2000.

Other resource to note

Smith, James Bryan, *A Spiritual Formation Workbook: Small-Group Resources for Nurturing Christian Growth*, HarperCollins, UK, 1999.